# THE
# LIFE-CHANGING

# POWER OF

### Tune In to Yourself,
### Transform Your Life

# INTUITION

## EMMA LUCY KNOWLES

ST. MARTIN'S
**ESSENTIALS**
**NEW YORK**

FOR ERIC AND LILY
AND THE "I AM"
THAT IS ALL OF US

Published in the United States by St. Martin's Essentials,
an imprint of St. Martin's Publishing Group

THE LIFE-CHANGING POWER OF INTUITION. Copyright © 2022 by Emma Lucy Knowles. All rights reserved. Printed in the United States of America. For information, address St. Martin's Publishing Group, 120 Broadway, New York, NY 10271.

www.stmartins.com

The Library of Congress Cataloging-in-Publication Data is available upon request.

ISBN 978-1-250-83784-4 (trade paperback)
ISBN 978-1-250-83785-1 (ebook)

Our books may be purchased in bulk for promotional, educational, or business use. Please contact your local bookseller or the Macmillan Corporate and Premium Sales Department at 1-800-221-7945, extension 5442, or by email at MacmillanSpecialMarkets@macmillan.com.

Originally published in the United Kingdom by Pop Press,
an imprint of Penguin Random House UK.

First U.S. Edition: 2022

10  9  8  7  6  5  4  3  2  1

# CONTENTS

INTRODUCTION                                          1

## 1.  UNDERSTANDING INTUITION                       16

## 2.  GETTING STARTED                               34

## 3.  EXPANDING YOUR PRACTICE                       66

## 4.  INTUITION FOR . . .                           130

## 5.  CARING FOR YOUR INTUITION                     194

CONCLUSION                                           241

RESOURCES AND FURTHER READING                        243

THANK YOU                                            245

INDEX                                                247

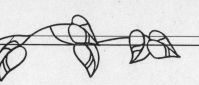

# THE STORY OF TWO WOLVES

A grandfather was teaching his grandson about life. . .

"A fight is going on inside me," he said to the boy. "It is a terrible fight and it is between two wolves."

"One is EVIL—he is anger, envy, sorrow, regret, grief, arrogance, self-pity, guilt, resentment, inferiority, lies, false pride, superiority, self-doubt and ego."

"The other is GOOD—he is joy, peace, love, hope, serenity, humility, kindness, benevolence, empathy, generosity, truth, compassion and faith."

"This same fight is going on inside you, and inside every other person, too."

The grandson thought about it for a minute and then asked his grandfather, "Which wolf will win?"

The grandfather simply replied, "The one you feed."

# INTRODUCTION

You've probably felt the power of your own intuition far more than you realize. Perhaps you haven't been able to name it because you can't see, touch or hear it. Or perhaps you know it as something different—it may feel to you like a gut instinct or pull. Or a kind of instinctive knowing but you can't work out precisely where this knowing and its all seeing wisdom comes from. However it feels to you, you are now ready to claim it as your own and use as your greatest guide for living and leading your life!

So, HUGE CONGRATULATIONS! You've hit that sweet spot of change where you know within you that there is "more" out there. It's a feeling that you have, alongside an inner awareness, that you are far more powerful than you—and others—give you credit for, and that you have the ability to harness and control more than you have been led to believe. Perhaps you've become tired and frustrated from wandering around in the dark, not being able to pinpoint why, and to that I say GOOD! It's time to dive in and teach yourself (yes, IN-TUITION is moving inward to teach yourself) something that can change and even heal your life on all levels—be it emotionally, mentally and/or physically.

# We are the creators of our lives

You are your greatest superpower—if there is one thing you should take from this book, it is this. It's not just a punchy slogan or an Instagram post, it's the truth. My intuition tells me you've picked up this book because you are curious about your inner power, that inner voice—your intuition. That you are ready to learn, to explore and grow . . . to empower yourself to your fullest potential!

The good news is, as in all things intuition, you don't need to worry or wait for the right teacher to arrive because YOU are your teacher. That's exciting news, but maybe it's also slightly terrifying because no one can teach you how to be you. Sure they can guide you but, let me tell you that in this sense, you are your greatest guide—please remember that life only shapes us and we have the power to learn and unlearn what's holding us back from knowing and honoring who we truly are.

If you feel that you are not ready to trust yourself or love yourself the best that you can right now, worry not. To take that much responsibility on, you need a hand to hold and that's all part of the process. Reaching out to intuition is about learning to trust yourself, which in turn is about self-love!

Listen to your intuition— it's on your side.

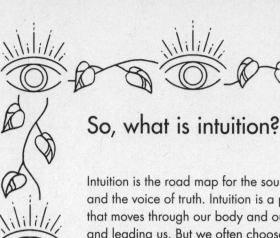

# So, what is intuition?

Intuition is the road map for the soul, our most reliable guide and the voice of truth. Intuition is a powerful second breath that moves through our body and our being, silently guiding and leading us. But we often choose not to listen to intuition or become disconnected from it, allowing its voice to become crowded out by the noise of modern life, our ego and its fears.

Despite all this, we will still catch echoes of our intuition. It's that soft and subtle voice that whispers to you, often disguised as your own, the voice within you that you never quite learned to trust because they don't teach that at school (and they really should!). It's that gut reaction or that "kick in the gut," sent as if by magic to guide you to what you need and away from what you don't.

## INTUITION IS OUR SILENT SUPER-NAVIGATOR

Our intuition is an intellect, a power, an energy that uses our whole body and its senses as its muscle, mind and voice. Intuition is not just for the special or the few. We all are intuitive, each and every one of us, and the secret to understanding it comes from learning what it means to you. By connecting with it, speaking to it, nurturing and developing your relationship with it, just as you would with a beloved friend, it will become your greatest strength, come rain or shine.

Our intuition can, more often than not, feel like something that remains dormant until something painful or shocking crosses our path and our ability to understand its power, and decipher its language, increases exponentially, almost out of nowhere in that moment. We become somewhat superhuman, empowered and elated, as it holds us lovingly in its grip while we power through the crisis.

Now this may sound dramatic, but intuition tends to come to full force in the middle of a crisis. That's most likely when and how you will first remember hearing or feeling it at its feistiest—when something just doesn't feel right. It sings louder the closer to the edge you are getting because that's when it needs your attention urgently! "Step away from that decision, Emma, that is baaaad news right there," and it's right, of course. Then, like a loyal dog it seems to settle back sleepily by your side. You might even think that it's just vanished back into the thin air that you thought it came from until you are in need of it again and, guess what, there it will be.

But also like our loyal fluffy companions, the more effort and attention you apply to training and loving it, the stronger it will become, and not just at guarding you in the bad times when you are "at the edge," but also guiding you with the same level of love and respect that you have shown it through every day of your life.

It's a super-computer that patiently waits for you to learn how to read, listen and then respond to it and, much as our abs need a good old gym session in order to get stronger, we must train our intuitive muscle!

When there is so much going on in our modern lives, how do we work out what feels right from what feels wrong? How do we learn to trust our intuition and become more in tune with who we really are and what we really need? Learning to work with your intuition can help you heal your past, make peace with your present and create your future.

At school we are taught about the intricacy of how our beautiful bodies function—all those intelligent networks and structures, growing, repairing and healing without needing instruction from our mind. It's like breathing—we don't need to tell ourselves to "breathe in, breathe out." It's the same with intuition and its system of working—over time, you won't need to sit every day and connect to it in order to ask questions of it.

# Tapping into the universe and its energy

Our intuition is more than a force within us or a mechanical tool like our breathing apparatus. Our intuition has a higher connective force—it connects to the universal energy and light that surrounds us and feeds and fuels our own life force, just like the breath we take from the atmosphere around us. Our intuition can move beyond our mind, beyond our body. It is a super-connecter that allows us to flow our energy and light to communicate and connect with the great energy of the universe—the higher power, spirit or god, however that is known to you. Intuition taps into this universal knowing or voice of truth and receives guidance for our highest good. We can heal our energy, our light and our physical, mental and emotional body to bring in all that is happy, healthy and healing to us.

We can also use our intuition to make connections with other human beings, jobs, events or places whose energy aligns with our own vibe and we can go one step further— we can use this super-connection to draw in or manifest what is for our highest good or the highest good of others, and equally let go of all that holds us back.

Allow yourself to feel the universal energy, your life force. I want to teach you how to understand and tap into it, to feel comfortable and safe within it, whatever your personal faith or beliefs. I like to think of this greater force in the same way we view the internet—we cannot see it, but it is all around us and it can bring us great wisdom and light. But unlike our belief in the internet, we often struggle to believe and have faith in this greater force, much as we mistrust our own intuition and energy.

# How intuition can help you

Most of us will have felt a special connection with our intuition as kids when, hand in hand, we explored, we learned and were open to listening to that beyond which our human eyes allowed us to see. Some people may call that playing make-believe, but I say that at this time in our lives we were the super-creators—big thinkers without limitation. But as we grew up, we simply forgot this truth and the ensuing years of social conditioning taught us a different way of learning, of thinking, of "knowing."

As adults, we're told to find experts to give us answers rather than seeking guidance within ourselves. Over time we replace the child's insistent cry of "But why?" with an exhausted acceptance that it "just is" and we learn how to follow the line as a social pattern or of another's ego as a shortcut to an "easy life." Little do we know what a rod for our back we are creating. Most importantly, it has left us believing that we cannot trust ourselves, instead of believing in and honoring ourselves.

As a kid (ain't hindsight a wonderful thing!!) I should have listened to my inner voice on cooling my ego and creating my future from my own playbook, but there was certainly no book in the school library, no handy set of instructions given out in class that could have helped me with this. It's only when I turned thirty that I realized the book that I needed to read didn't come bound with a handy contents page, but that I was in fact my own book filled with information and a teacher in my intuition who spoke a language I didn't know I needed to understand. So, my lesson to you is that you are your own teacher, you and your intuition hand in hand as one.

So, why learn about intuition? Well, consider that you want to go to Spain on holiday, but when there, you feel you would have got so much more from the trip if you knew more about its traditions, culture or the language. How much more clear-sighted would you have felt? It's the same with intuition—it's a silent language used the world over that gives us a means of experiencing a whole new depth or angle of our life and of the world around us. It makes it all the more enriching and fulfilling, not just on big trips or life events, but in the everyday.

For me, my intuition has saved my skin—and in more ways than one and more times than I can now remember. It has helped me out of a relationship that was not good for me (and yes that's an understatement), where I lost all sight of myself, missed all the warning signs from intuition and spirit— until one day intuition and spirit gave me the kick I needed right in the gut to leave.

I took my intuition by the reins (or rather I let it take me by the reins) and I started to listen in—properly this time—to what people were really saying and what they needed, beyond the words they spoke. I learned how not to take things so personally— to understand what was mine and what was everyone else's (energetically and emotionally). I became more confident, more trusting in people, in myself and in my intuition and the more I trusted, the more my intuition and I grew together . . . and so did my career!

Through developing my relationship with intuition, I developed a clearer relationship with my wants and needs. I would work with my intuition to ask if a particular food resonated with me or if it would make me feel bloated or unwell. Then I expanded that practice to find what I really needed in friendships—I'd ask who fills me up, what puts me down? With relationships, I look at what's on offer and I ask whether it's good for me, rather than simply accepting what was put before me as I had so many times before.

And over time and the more you commit to your intuition, you will see how you attract the right people with the right energy and the right situations for you, for your highest good. Life becomes easier, you feel freer and more confident in yourself and able to see clearly what doesn't serve you, so you can walk away from it if necessary, and sooner rather than later!

I should take a moment to elaborate here—I talk a lot about the "highest good" within these pages so let me explain what that means. Firstly, there is always a scale in life, right? How happy are you from one to ten right now? How good does something make you feel on a scale of one to ten? This is the most important scale, for we can be in a good situation or relationship, but we've compromised—we're perhaps at four out of ten, but we tell ourselves we're at an eight, thereby denying ourselves the top reaches of the scale. In effect, we believe ourselves to be happy with our lot because that's what we deserve and we start to talk ourselves down or sell ourselves short. When we do something for our highest good, that doesn't always mean it will be easy, but it means that we will be caring for ourselves at the highest level.

Often as human beings, we get stuck at a level of "wanting." I am not saying you shouldn't want the best for yourself, but there is a difference between wanting and needing. When we fixate on wanting the car or the partner that looks a certain way we are looking from an ego-led viewpoint. We reject an opportunity or person because they didn't look or appear the way our mind "wanted." Our highest self is that part of us that connects our intuition to the universe and spirit. It's that part of you that knows what is truly best for you and will have the best outcome for you (even though you may not be able to see it yet through human eyes) and it won't just provide you and your ego with a quick hit of "feel-good" that comes as quickly as it goes.

With our intuition we can take control of situations, relationships and even our thoughts. It provides clarity and a fresh, healthy perspective. Walking with intuition has showed me to learn how to quieten the mind, calm the anxiety and still the worries—even when it feels the world is exploding all around us. As I said, tough things still happen—we cannot stop all of life's hard learning—but we can learn how to call for intuition at these times and how to trust its guidance to help show us the best way through.

# How to use this book

This book is inspired by two things. The first is the people
I have had the pleasure of guiding along on their healing journey
in my practice and the work we do together. My clients often
say they wish we had more time together, that they could make
the feelings from the session last, to take me home and digest
everything I know and to lean into that knowledge as and when
they need. Well, here you go!

  The second is to create a toolkit for anyone who wants
to use their intuition a bit more wisely, as a guide in everyday
life sure, but also as a powerful light in tough times. This
book is a celebration of your voice, your journey, your adventure
and mission, a map and a guide to help you develop
and strengthen your intuition muscle, for you to work out
at your own pace, using the lens of your own personal
experience.

Your intuition is powerful and so, my friend, are you.

In this book you will learn how to:

• Tap into the secret of changing your life that is already
  inside you.
• Connect with your intuition and let it become your greatest
  compass and navigator.
• Feel, listen and know just what intuition is to you, and what
  it isn't.

- Listen to your intuition to nourish your dreams, calm your mind, open your soul and help you achieve your goals in life, work and love.
- Create a greater connection with your authentic self and attract positive energy, circumstances and people into your life, and learn how to lovingly let go of what no longer serves you (and perhaps never did).
- Trust your inner wisdom and heal your fears, stresses and anxieties.

We will fill your intuitive toolkit with:

- Practical exercises and meditations to help you sharpen your intuition so that you feel more grounded, fulfilled and self-loving.
- Energy and spiritual practices to support your development and growth.
- Practices and exercises to release lingering thoughts in the mind that have an energetical effect on the body over time.
- Ways to care for your intuition and in turn care for and heal yourself, as well as ways to trust in your intuition and yourself in times of doubt and anxiety.

Intuition will be your guide and your teacher, and today it's teaching you how to wake up, to throw off years of conditioning that has left you believing that real power is material that can be bought or traded, and comes with a hierarchy to climb or a battle to be fought. Because of this conditioning, intuition will feel like a punch or an emotional bullet (and that's no bad thing!) when you first open yourself up to it after so many years of hanging out with your old pal ego, which has diluted intuition's voice and power (more on this to follow).

I would like you to see this book as a series of exercises set to awaken your intuition in order to find empowerment, faith and confidence in your true self. Use, reject, rework and retry each exercise as many times as you need, BUT always ask yourself in that process, "How does this feel for me?" or "why is this frustrating me?" before you reject it. When you feel frustrated know your pal ego is simply trying to pull your mental reins back into its law and order—so take a rest from it, move to a different section and come back to it later. And when ego starts chatting back to you (and it will!), questioning whether you are getting from these pages what you WANT (rather than need), simply ask your intuition "What am I missing?" and "What do I need to see that ego is blurring?" It will always answer, we just need to learn how to hear, so let's do that.

So, here we are, a book wholeheartedly written to and for you. Sound good? Then there's no time to be lost. Let me introduce you to intuition!

*rolls my
third eye

1

# UNDERSTANDING INTUITION

Much like learning to drive a car, there is a little theory to learn before we can jump into the driver's seat and pull away from the curb. We are all born with intuition. Intuition is an intelligence. It's a body of energy or light and, most importantly, it is a huge part of who we are. In fact, the more we nourish and feed our intuition and the more we get to know that "part" of ourselves, the more complete, connected and whole—the more alive—we will begin to feel.

Intuition is not separate from us. It is an energy that breathes within and alongside us, an extension of our truest selves. A sixth sense, if you like, that uses body language such as the hairs on your arms and at the back of your neck to tell us what and who we can trust; what we should and shouldn't do or be.

It resides within us but it is by no means a lazy house guest because its purpose is to connect us with our deepest and truest desires, when conceived for our highest good (remember that one?), and how to bring them into actuality. Intuition is not acquired; like happiness and love, it cannot be bought. What can be learned, however, is how we uncover it and how we use it.

Intuition is a power and like all power, it can be almighty and It can also be soft and gentle. There Is no right or wrong, black or white. Don't fear its reaction—it will never tell you off or punish you. Its purpose is to guide you.

Intuition is smart; it is kind, loving and speaks to us in many languages, not just those that come in words. It uses our own physical multisensory network as its vehicle in order to connect you to your highest/greatest self and potential. Intuition is more than words; it's more than feelings and emotions. It's an almost invisible force that precedes the invention of language and is as old and true as time itself. Above all else, it is yours, to be defined by you, without needing anyone else's approval!

Intuition provides us with a bluetooth connection to the world, to the universe. It connects us to an energy beyond ourselves—all you need to do is to tune into the wavelength to deepen your connectivity.

It does not require a religious practice to activate or support it, but it can be used to enhance a spiritual or alternative faith, or mindful or meditative practice.

For the fact seekers or the naysayers among you, science has shown that intuition does indeed exist, with studies having successfully measured our intuition. For example, research carried out by Joel Pearson, the associate professor of psychology at the University of New South Wales in Australia, not only showed that intuition helped participants make better decisions under the right circumstances, but that they did so with greater confidence . . . amen to that!

Intuition sings through our body, so it's crucial that we tend to our body, which is our intuition's vessel. The stronger the body, the stronger the receptors and the sharper and quicker we can take heed of the intuitive call.

Finally, practice and patience makes perfect—you will get better at working with and trusting your intuition over time.

"Told you so."
Sincerely,
your Intuition.

# Intuition, Ego and Fear

I have feared my intuition and avoided its truth. I have been skeptical, sometimes I still can be, in healthy doses. My ego has needed to prove it wrong. My fear has undermined it and my want has driven me to impatience. Welcoming in intuition has revolutionized my life and my relationships, in the process making me a better and more understanding human being, who is at peace with being a forever work in progress rather than a fixed being.

What do I mean by ego and fear? Ego feels like a big sugar hit—tasty in the moment but its high doesn't last long. Intuition, on the other hand, teaches in many guises and its feeling is good and lasting. It may not always come in such spiked awareness, so don't give up on it if it sometimes feels harder to achieve than ego's desires or if the feel-good doesn't come with instant gratification.

Ego isn't a big fan of intuition, but it's not its enemy either. It's just that ego likes to keep us "safe," where it is "comfortable," whereas our intuition wants the best for us, so ego is scared of where intuition can take us and that can make ego feel all shades of out of control. Ego uses tough language, harsh words and fear to keep us in line. Intuition uses love to guide us. We have grown in a material world, we are taught to reach for material goals and for material gain. We have been bathing in and speaking ego's language from day dot and we have been taught to "want" so the "want," the "I" (which is the language of the ego) is all too present in our every day: "buy this," "do this," "be better." The more we hear this voice, the louder it gets and the more power and control our ego gains, the quieter intuition becomes and the less we lean into what provides us with love and kindness.

Now ego and fear can be useful tools on our journey—we can use them as tells or markers that we are stepping outside our comfort zone (which is useful and also a very good thing!) so we know that we need to make time to heal a particular way that we think about ourselves or see life. This book will work to show you where ego has become the dominant voice and where it might have kept you on a narrow path.

For example, have you done or said something and then later regretted that action, saying "I wish I'd trusted my gut," "Why didn't I listen to myself" or "I knew that." That is a sign that ego has influenced your actions rather than intuition, but also a sign that you are already feeling intuition but aren't fully trusting it yet. Ego and its friend, fear, succeeded in making you doubt yourself and your intuition, and kept you where it believes you'll be safe—and we should of course thank it for that, but now walk on from it back to intuition's loving arms.

It's important to note that the mind hears ego through a loudhailer. Ego lives in and is part of the mind, whereas intuition moves through the entire body. We therefore tend to trust what is being amplified from the mind as it feels louder and clearer to us—again, at school, most of the day is spent diving into our mind and not our heart and gut.

We can trust our intuition to be the true key to problem-solving but we have to listen without fear and understand the battle with the wants of our ego.

Trust the vibes you get, energy doesn't lie.

## EGO VS INTUITION—THE VOICE WITHIN

So now we know the antithesis of intuition is ego and its dear pal fear. Although intuition is by definition more than words, we can use words to pinpoint which thoughts and feelings are driven by ego and which are drawn forth by intuition—I am a BIG fan of lists so here's a short one for you to compare and contrast (feel free to add your own entries):

| INTUITION | VS | EGO |
|---|---|---|
| Spiritual | | Human |
| Belief | | Doubt |
| Need | | Want |
| Love | | Hate |
| Growth | | Sabotage/destruction |
| Kindness | | Anger |
| Compassion | | Greed |
| Wholeness | | I |
| Us | | Me |
| Try me | | Why me |

## HOW TO SEE BETWEEN INTUITION AND EGO

My intuition has often come at its clearest while I'm running or in the shower . . . when my mind is at its most free, undistracted by the daily mental churn and chatter. So, my best advice to you is to free your mind and intuition will follow and this book will show you how. Here are a few healthy guidelines to help you find your path as we clear the way.

Intuition should not be used to hurt, trick or trap another. Smugness is the friend of ego, not intuition. Intuition should be used to better ourselves and our experience and invite others to do the same, not to tell another to change, nor to call someone out for being "dishonest" or a "drain"—we are all only human and are all on our own journey, moving at our own pace—so for those not ready for that part of the path—forgive them, even from a distance, and carry on your way.

Intuition is magic in a sense but not the sort of magic that just leads you to what you think you want and on your clock (remember time too is man-made!). If it leads you away from a relationship or friendship that your ego wants because it's safe, you need to be brave and look deeper, hand in hand with your intuition, at the true nature of that relationship. Is your intuition niggling at you to move from a "bad" or "toxic" relationship or a job that ego has seen as solid because it fills our material standards—or those of other people? Although the change from old habits, patterns and relationships looks hard at first, intuition will work with you and lighten your load.

Intuition tells the truth (ouch!) and is sometimes brutally honest (especially when you are missing or ignoring the point) but it is always for the love of you. That isn't always easy to hear, but we have to commit to hearing the good, the bad and the ugly in order to better ourselves.

Sometimes our mind gets lost or distracted by the noise and the hunger of the ego's wants and the fear of our past endeavors. Like intuition, ego is clever and it also uses the voices of the mind, but negatively. Ego says you can't; intuition says you can, but perhaps not this way . . . Ego says, "I want," intuition says, "I should." Ego says you are useless and battles you with crippling doubt; intuition encourages you and shows that you are more than enough and to come as you are.

It is hard to trust what you can't see. Ego knows that too, so we will work through this to reach the sweet and all-seeing intuitive spot—your mind's eye (also known as your third eye) to help you know what you can trust.

That being said, we are not to blame for our ego and fear. They are useful tools but we need to take them by the hand and walk with them, to talk to and challenge them—not be chained to and led by them.

Finally, and most importantly, sometimes what stunts our intuition is our impatience to prove it right . . . please keep that front of mind as we go!

Intuition encourages
you to come as
you are.

# How to Honor
# Your Superpower

Our intuition must be handled with care. It is there for the good of all, not for the good of your ego, so before you begin your intuitive work, you must commit to parking your ego right here and right now . . . you good with that? You have to be ready to ensure that you are coming from a place of kindness, wholeness and love, rather than fear, vengeance, envy, material gain or with the need to feel vindicated or to prove someone right or wrong.

## GRATITUDE IS ALWAYS THE ATTITUDE

You know that feeling—when your boss or a loved one only seems to focus on the things you haven't delivered on, rather than what you have actually achieved? Demotivating, isn't it? You feel undervalued and a little deflated. Well, intuition also needs to be shown some love and for you to recognize the good work it's doing for you, not just in bringing to you what you desire, but in guiding and protecting you, and creating with you.

Take the time to count your blessings and give gratitude for where you are and what you have right now because it's the key for firing your intuitive engine (more on that on page 46). A really healthy habit to form is to give your intuition and yourself a little daily review—it's like a happy hug for the soul. Start in the morning by focusing on the good in your life, even if you initially feel there's not too much to be happy about—

you will find that there always is. List ten things (as a minimum) that you are grateful for—be it in a journal or on the list function on your smartphone, let's put tech to good work! It can be a simple word or a sentence, in thanks for something someone did for you today, the sun shining in the skies or for your home or your health—don't limit your list, let it flow. You could give thanks to people who do the jobs that you benefit from, perhaps those you so rarely think about—our health service, street cleaners and bus drivers always make my list.

Fixing your mind on a state of abundance and moving away from a state of lack makes a healthy channel for your daily intuitive flow. You will be tapping into your intuition's favorite frequency—that of joy, love and positive intent, clearing the mental airwaves so that you can hear and feel your intuitive calls with more clarity.

Take the time to count your blessings and give gratitude.

2

•

# GETTING
# STARTED

•

So, here we go—it's time to rouse the power that lies, as always, within you. In this next section you will learn about tapping into your intuition and its toolkit—creating somewhere safe and supportive to explore the intuitive exercises and practices that follow as well as using energy tools such as crystals to heighten intuition's voice and connect with your highest self.

Before you turn the page, I know from personal experience that it will sound like there is a lot of prep to be done and patience required to connect and explore—but really there's not: don't let ego fool you with the word count! Just like warming up for a run or packing your bag for the day ahead, it's important to be as prepared and warmed up as possible to get the best results: in this case healthy habits that over time will make your intuition come to you as easy and naturally as breathing. What I am really saying is please do not hop, skip and jump the prep and practice because this is half the work and it can be so much
fun. Just watch how and ask why ego is trying to hold you back by putting this off "to tomorrow" or "to another day . . ."

Trust me when I say, it's important to take time to build your sacred space, so that intuition and spirit know where to meet you and so that you can enjoy the benefits of simply walking into this space and feeling its benefits come rain or shine. Commit to leaning into and learning your tells and don't beat yourself up if you miss a day or two—this is learning but not school and life happens in between.

Now, please, go play!

# Creating a
# Sacred Space

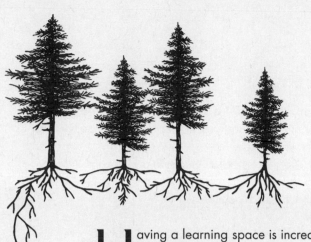

Having a learning space is incredibly important in your intuitive workings; the stillness, calm and quiet that you will invite into and harness in such a space are crucial companions so that you feel confident to trust in yourself and your intuitive connection.

Sacred spaces have been made in many practices across the ages in places of worship, in spiritual or tribal grounds, but also out in nature, in art galleries and most importantly at home. As with intuition, it should be unique to you. My dad, for example, who seeks connection to his intuition through "the great architect in the sky," finds his sacred space walking along the river. I too sometimes find it on the riverfront but while pounding out a morning run. I have also come to know that if I have had a bad day, the first place I want to be is at home. Not the bricks and mortar of the house, but the loving energy nested within it. This is the place that gives me comfort: a safe, loving, sacred space. All you need to do is to find your own space of specific focus and intention, just as you'd create a space to sleep peacefully in or where you'd sit calmly to unwind and come back to self.

The first place to start is by asking yourself, and indirectly your intuition, a few questions to scope out its placement, its home within your home:

Which room in my home best suits my growth? Which part of that room? Where am I most comfortable? Where do I get/find the most peace?

- Ask "yourself" does light help me relax? For example, when I sit near a window do I feel more chilled, or do I want somewhere where the lighting is softer or darker, somewhere that helps me to zone in?
- Ask yourself whether you prefer to sit on the floor or on a chair.
- Keep exploring what makes you feel at peace, allows you to feel most "held" so that you can let go in this space and properly surrender.

## ONCE YOU HAVE LOCATED YOUR SPACE

For now, the most important thing you need in this space is a chair or a cushion on the floor, whatever feels comfortable. Clear away anything that feels like it's clogging you—make space for yourself, literally. You can use a table, a shelf or a bookcase for holding the "things," the totems that I suggest next, before you or at eye level.

I believe all healing and protective energy is love and comes from a peaceful nature, which is why I like to add these feelings, these vibes to a sacred space, by bringing in people I love or places I find peace in. Consider if you would like to add a photo of your loved ones or a picture of that mind-blowing view from your last trip to the beach or of your favorite coastline. Perhaps there is a teddy bear that you snuggled yourself to sleep with as a kid or something that represents your beliefs—a statue of your god or goddess or a heart-shaped rock you found on the beach that represents love to you. Ask yourself, what is it that provokes those feelings of warmth and love within? Then start to add these tokens of love and peace to your sacred space so that when you sit here, you know you are sitting here safely, in love and peace, with the right strength of energy to support your journey.

We will also use crystals throughout the book to support the energy or to use as a talisman—a reminder of the intentions you will start to set throughout these pages. We will also use the flame of a candle to assist us in focusing, meditating and tuning in more deeply, so allow this space to grow as you and your intuition do—there's no need to rush just to get it done.

Your space will grow as you do, it may even move. That's fine. Let it guide you. And we will delve even deeper into that starting on page 58.

# Connecting to Your Intuition

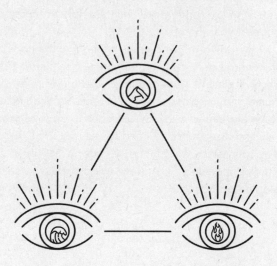

L et's say a big old hello to your body, which in all its glory is like a super-computer for intuition—it reacts and responds in self-defense, from habit and instinct for sure, but it also has "tells" that you must learn to read. These tells are powerful tools for intuitive communication. We often think of these in the negative when you feel that someone is not speaking or enacting the whole truth—perhaps their mouth quivers and we say "Ah-ha, they're lying, they always do that when they're lying" or in poker when we try to catch someone out, but let's hit pause and iron this out. Let me reiterate—intuition is not about winning or about being right. It isn't about other people, it's about you, so let's bring it all back to you—back to and into the body.

Our intuition sings throughout our entire body and just as we can supercharge the engine of our car with a few modifications and tweaks made with precision and care, we too can fine-tune our body to become alert to not only respond and read our intuition, but to ask of it too.

The first exercise is given to help you to become aware of just how your intuition speaks through your body—how it sends signals and signs through your entire being. We call these your tells, or body indicators, and they can be so subtle but at times so forceful, ranging from anything from an itch in your hand to a deep pulse in your belly. We will learn how to sit with your body in order to learn what your intuitive tells are, but also to choose (by listening and deciding with your intuition), "What's my INTUITIVE YES?" and "What's my INTUITIVE NO?," so that you can then build on that to ask your intuition simply at any time "What do I need?," "What do I need to step away from?." Throughout the book, we will explore how to ask your intuition, "What do I need to do?" so it becomes as natural as when you listen to your tummy when it grumbles.

●

It isn't about other people, it's about you, so let's bring it all back to you—back to and into the body.

●

# FINDING YOUR TELLS

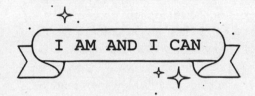

I AM AND I CAN

We have to work hard and steadily in order to develop our "What's my . . ." tells so if you are a keen beam in the morning, do this practice then, but if you are a bright night owl, get into this before your head hits the pillow—always practice in your safe or sacred space while we are growing and developing your skills.

## DAY ONE:
### "WHAT'S MY INTUITIVE YES?"

Do this exercise seated on the floor, on a chair, beanbag or a cushion— whatever is comfy for you—and set this in your sacred space. Comfort is key and you should support your back and neck—a rigid body will create a rigidity of mind which will seep into your intuitive flow. But when I say comfortable, be supported upright rather than lying down as this will help your focus, your alertness and in turn your awareness of your intuition— intuitive practice and play is also extremely relaxing, so you don't want to lie down and fall into a slumber . . .

Your breath is your guide and it will be the key throughout the book to start your intuitive engine. On the other hand, technological flow (computers, smartphones or watches) get in the way when working with these vibes, so put your phone on airplane mode and use it as your timer. If crystals are your thing, shungite crystal is epic at zapping technological interference from your energy field.

Aim to do this exercise for six minutes a day, for six days over one week. If you miss a few days, don't beat yourself up. Nothing is ever lost if you've invested time in it, but life does sometimes interrupt you. Commit to it with an open heart and you'll find it more fun and freeing; avoid treating it like a chore or as a fixed and tethered plan.

So lets set a timer for six minutes (if you only have four minutes no problem; if you have ten, go for it!). For your first few tries, read the instructions as set out opposite aloud or in your mind as you go—it will help you to focus. Note down what you see, what you feel, and any other miniature sensations you would ordinarily overlook. As you start these exercises, read through them as a guide or record yourself talking through the steps, creating your own audio guide. I know there is a lot to take in but trust me—the more you do and the more you invest, the more intuition will guide you, the less your mind will need to do and the less chance that your ego will have to get involved.

**1/**
Come to the breath, watch and feel the breath in your body. Have your palms turned faced up and open— this is a sign to the universe and to your intuition that you are ready and open to receiving. Use the breath now to feel for and find your flow. Start to visualize and feel that you are drawing the breath in from the base of your feet, right up and through the body, breathing out through the top of the head (your crown chakra/energy center).

**2/**
As you repeat, allow any tension or worry to move from the body or the breath and into the earth beneath you and out of your way. I emphasize slowly here—give yourself at least six rounds of cleansing, grounding breaths as you connect back to yourself, to your spirit and to create and awaken the space as you connect with the intention of knowing and trusting in your intuition and it in you.

**3/**
Now we come to speak to intuition and to ask of it "What is my YES?" Over time you can shape this question for deeper clarity, but to avoid overloading youself at the beginning of your practice, let's start by stripping it right back. Keep it simple and ask, "What is my YES, what is my positive?"

**4/**
You can say this aloud or in your mind, with eyes closed or open. You can write this on a cue card and focus your vision on it, but all you need to do is ask. Allow your breath to carry you, to move that question around your body and your being as you await your intuitive response. Connect and ground that energy with the earth as you take your breath and awareness to your feet once again, Inhale and ask, "What is my YES?" Raise that question to the heavens on your breath, moving that breath up along the legs, along the spine up into the heart. As you exhale through the top of your head, now ask, "What is my positive?" Repeat 3 times.

**5/**
You may be visual, you may be led by feelings (you're likely both but at different times) and your intuition will sense this and respond in kind. With

every breath you surrender to your intuition, it starts to gear your body to respond to the ask and to find a way to show you the answer to your call. For me, my "What's my YES, what's my positive?" is a prickle or a vibration that my intuition runs down my left arm or sometimes in my left palm. For another client, it's a rush of a cool breeze up their spine, while for another it's a visual image seen in her mind's eye—an image of her smiling and winking back or blowing a kiss at herself. Don't limit yourself to how another defines it—there is no right, wrong or weird, so allow yourself to feel it. Watch as your intuition creates the scenario in your mind's eye, your third eye. The part of your body it is emanating from is your alarm bell, your tell or feel, and allow for that level of reaction in your own way and in your own body. Tune in deeper, by using your breath to sink into and open up the vision or the feeling, to what word or sound intuition is whispering on the wind around your ears, not in your mind— there is a notable difference. Trust it. And if your mind should say "I can't" or "You're doing this WRONG" come back to the breath—state to

yourself "I am and I can" and come back to asking.

6/

Sometimes this will come like a bolt of lightning for the first time—a big "aha" moment. Sometimes it's more subtle and you may discount it—please don't. Note it down because this will build over time—remember this is an exercise in trust and patience—that's why we spend six days watching how this shows and grows, how it develops and how it becomes more of us so that we can learn to trust it.

DAY TWO:
"WHAT'S MY INTUITIVE NO?"

On day two, we move back to the breath as in day one but now we ask of intuition, "What's my intuitive NO, what is my step away from?" It's the same process, but this may be easier to reveal or it may be harder. If it is harder, accept that and don't allow yourself to feel frustration as that leads us back to ego, back to fear. This is not instant gratification but a slow, day-by-day build.

Come back to the breath, come back to the body. Have fun with it— allow the body and mind to clear with the breath and then come to ask, and watch and listen. Note down what you see, what you feel, and any other miniature sensations you would ordinarily overlook; any time you feel "stuck" or like you can't—come back to affirm "I am and I can." That mantra has saved me from many an ego's dance in fear.

## 1/

Come to the breath, palms face up once more and open to receiving. Use the breath to feel for and find your flow and start to visualize and feel that you are drawing the breath in from the base of your feet up and through the body, breathing out through the top of the head (your crown chakra/energy center).

## 2/

As you repeat, the tension from the body will start to dissipate gently and slowly. It will be taken by your breath, away from the body and grounded into the earth or rise to the heavens. Give yourself at least six rounds of breath as you connect back to yourself, to your spirit and awaken the space for your intuition to rise out toward you as you connect with the intention of knowing and in trusting each other.

## 3/

Speak to your intuition and ask of it, "What is my NO? What's my 'move away from'?" As before, you can shape this question for deeper clarity over time, but start by keeping it simple.

## 4/

Say it aloud or in your mind, with eyes closed or open. Write it down on a cue card and focus your vision on it, but all you need to do is ask. Allow your breath to carry you, to move that question around your body and your being. Connect and ground that energy to the earth by taking your breath, your awareness and attention to the base of your feet—breathing in as you ask, "What is my NO?" Raise that question to the heavens as you exhale through the top of your crown, now asking, "What is my step away from?"

5/

With every breath surrender to your intuition. Watch as your intuition creates the scenario in your mind's eye, your third eye. The part of your body it is emanating from is your alarm bell, your tell or feel, and allow for that level of reaction in your own way and in your own body. Tune into this tell, this space, by using your breath to sink you deeper into the word, sound or visual that is whispering on the wind around your ears, not in your mind—there is a notable difference. Most importantly, feel it, see it, note it down.

### DAY THREE:
### AFFIRMING "WHAT'S MY YES?"

On day three we repeat our experience from day one and we return to deepen the feel of our "What's my YES, what's my positive?" to strengthening the message and our confidence in it. Be prepared for this tell to deepen rather than change, focus on the breath and the ask, rather than on what arrived the very first day you asked.

As ever . . . write it down! There is such power in logging your responses

even if you don't see it or feel that power yet—it will prove so useful!

### DAY FOUR:
### AFFIRMING "WHAT'S MY NO?"

On day four we repeat our practice from day two, to dial in deeper, to feel with more confidence "What's my NO, what's my step away from?" with an open mind as we surrender to what our intuition is telling, or showing us.

### DAY FIVE:
### COMBINING "YES" AND "NO" AND ESTABLISHING YOUR FAITH IN THEM

On day five we blend our "YES" with our "NO" and our "positive" and our "step away from" in exactly the same fashion. Repetition is key to strengthening not only the knowing, but also your belief and faith in it, so by the fifth day, your strength in your knowing has already grown and the feeling is becoming established.

PLEASE do not rush ahead—it is super-important you take this day by day because the deeper you connect, the deeper you trust. This means that when you come to call on your intuition out in the real world, you feel and you trust it because you just know it!

DAY SIX:
PLAYING WITH "WHAT'S MY YES?" AND "WHAT'S MY NO?"

So, you did it! You hit day six so come once more to our now comfortable, familiar seated position and fire your breath. Take six rounds of pure breath to sink you into your intuitive space and notice now how easy it is to move to this space within.

It's time to blend your tells, to expand your practice and release the brake from your intuitive flow—to move between your intuitive asks on your breath, so we will take two breaths, two inhalations and exhalations for each intuitive ask.

You inhale, you ask, "What's my YES, what's my positive?" and as you exhale, feel for the tell in your body, Breathe in again and ask, "What's my YES, what's my positive?" Exhale, allow and acknowledge the feeling in your body.

On your next inhale change the ask to "What's my NO, what's my step away from?" As you exhale feel it, acknowledge it, but don't over-pressure it. Repeat as you inhale and exhale once more.

Inhale and move back to "What's my YES, what's my positive?" This time we seek to feel the response as we inhale and as we exhale we ask, "What's my NO, what's my step away from?" We seek to feel the response within our body from our intuition as we ask—intuition doesn't need to wait to respond, it can and will call to you as soon as you open your mind to ask.

Play with this—gather your strength in the feeling and let your mind start to understand your new-found faith in your flow—your intuition. Play with it, use the above as a guide till the timer sounds and know that you are now in your flow, ready to take this out on the road.

TAKE IT UP ANOTHER GEAR

You can also expand the practice to ask, "What's my not now, not yet?" or "What's my play, what's my pause?" for when life isn't black and white, because remember that patience is key. Take it along the breath, work with and sit with intuition, follow the steps from day one and day two to expand your intuitive vocabulary and tells. Feel free to shape your own asks and use your intuition to look for the corresponding tells, but follow this process to ensure that your ego isn't stepping in to answer—remember it's all in how it feels and when it feels good it's your intuition. Trust yourself and your intuition. *You have got this.*

Come back to day six regularly to reset, realign and sharpen that intuitive connection. It's like keeping a friendship alive—to deepen the connection we need to pick the phone up, to dial back in and ask, "How's it feeling, how's it growing, how have we changed?" because it can change, you can change, life shifts and so too will your "YES," your "NO," your positive, your step away from. So, keep in touch with your intuition. Practice makes for a powerful tool and also a powerful craftsman in you.

This exercise is the foundation of all your intuitive work—it's a once-a-day practice that then becomes a once-a-week-practice and over time a once-a-month practice. Work through the steps in this exercise, dedicate one week to it as you start, build

your confidence in your tells, in your intuition and in yourself. Just as you need to keep your muscles toned, flexible and strong, you should seek to do this exercise once a week for a month to keep it fresh and alive within you, to continue to develop your confidence in your intuition and trust in yourself. We will build on this particular practice throughout the book so when we come to big asks such as "Is this job right for me?" your intuition can fire the signals into your "YES" or "NO" tell and you will feel and trust it without question—it'll prove invaluable.

Now you are working hand in hand with your intuition. Next you need to take little trips out with this new sense, just as you would build up to a marathon by taking longer and longer runs.

# FINDING YOUR TELLS
## at a glance

**Sit comfortably** in your sacred space—comfort is key.

**Set a timer** for 6 minutes.

**Come to the breath**—take 6 rounds of cleansing breath.

**Turn your palms** face up and open.

**Now we come to speak** to intuition and ask of it: "What is my yes/no?"

**Allow your breath to carry you** and move that question around your being as you await your intuitive response.

**On an inhale**, take your breath and awareness to your feet and ask, "What is my yes/no?" Raise that question to the heavens on your breath, moving it up along the legs, along the spine and up into the heart.

**As you exhale** through the top of your head, now ask "What is my positive/my step away from?" Repeat three times.

**Listen to your body** for your intuition's response—where do you feel confirmation? Trust it, write it down.

**If you feel you are not "getting it"** or your mind interferes, remember our mantra to blast those feelings away. Remember, "I am and I can."

# Taking Your Intuition
# Out For a Run

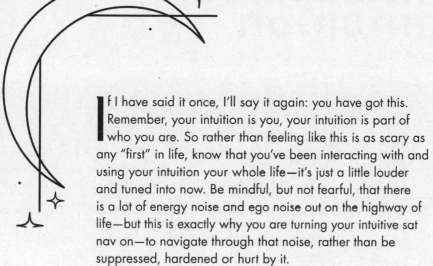

If I have said it once, I'll say it again: you have got this. Remember, your intuition is you, your intuition is part of who you are. So rather than feeling like this is as scary as any "first" in life, know that you've been interacting with and using your intuition your whole life—it's just a little louder and tuned into now. Be mindful, but not fearful, that there is a lot of energy noise and ego noise out on the highway of life—but this is exactly why you are turning your intuitive sat nav on—to navigate through that noise, rather than be suppressed, hardened or hurt by it.

Play with it as you grow and develop your skills, firstly with questions about yourself or something that's on your mind. Perhaps you want to ask whether this is the right job for me or whether this relationship or friendship is healthy for me? Should I commit to this trip? Should I invest in these shoes (yes, I use it for online shopping!)? You can ask of it whatever you need in order to delve deeper into your intuition and to understand your relationship with it.

And once again, (as if you need permission for it) have fun!

# ASKING YOUR INTUITION

Come back to the practice in the comfort of your sacred space. Set the timer for however long you need.

Take to the breath—six long cleansing breaths in total, moving that breath deep into the belly—closing your eyes as you come deeper within, but this time simply change what you are asking your intuition. We now trust our response, our intuitive tells to "What's my YES/what's my positive?" and "What's my NO, what's my step away from?"

As we ask on an inhale, we need to draw the question into our body, into our heart, in toward our intuition, so we inhale and ask, "Is this job right for me?" As we exhale, we move the ask deeper into our belly, deeper toward our intuition, "Should I go for it?"

Keep the question clear and simple, keep repeating it, moving it deeper into your body and being on every breath and then watch as your intuition starts to respond, using the awareness and the tells to "What's my YES?" or "What's my NO?" If you start to worry that you are getting this "wrong" or that you "can't do this" or "can't feel it," know you are hearing your ego, so take a break and come back to it in half an hour or even later in the day. Eventually you and your intuition will be so tightly synced that it becomes stronger than the voice of your ego.

Keep going with these intuitive exercises. Soon you'll be able to listen to your intuition without needing to be in your sacred space and you will be able to tune in while in the office or while standing in the shop. You'll be able to use your breath to carry the ask on the go, just by visualizing being in your sacred space. Keep practicing—when someone texts you to ask whether you want to come out tonight or if you are deciding whether to treat yourself to a new pair of shoes. The question doesn't matter, what is important is that you practice the ask and feeling for the tell. These small, seemingly "unimportant" asks will give you the confidence to trust your intuition when you feel you are on the edge of a monumental game change. As you are reading this you may think "this is impossible"—say hello and then a short goodbye to your ego . . . KNOW that you can and dive right into it!

This is important—please always ask yourself if you are hoping for your answer to be a yes when your intuition is saying no. Sometimes ego will seem to "win out" but it's only momentary. Do not throw in the towel when that happens—I've created a section of hacks (see page 106) to get you back into the ring, back to your flow because trust me, I still have those days now . . .

# Introducing Elemental Power and Expanding Your Sacred Space

ntuition always leads me back to the earth and to Mother Nature, just as much as it leads me up to the universe and into the heavens. It leads me to consider how we, each individual, is a tiny planet in ourselves on this beautiful big planet Earth and that leads me to look at what nourishes our glorious earth. I look at what the earth is made of, what feeds her, fuels her atmosphere, and then I start to use that to invest deeper, to enrich and grow my own planet, my body, my being. So, what is she made of? What makes the earth turn and thrive, and what within that can assist us in doing the same? It's the elements of earth, air, fire and water.

As you've come to see, I also always recommend breath work in our intuitive practices (for it represents the element air). Tapping into the power of breath makes an unconditional space within the body for the universe, spirit and, most importantly, our intuition to flow through and fill. Not only this, but tapping into the breath allows us to access the parasympathetic nervous system, relaxing the body, the muscles, the organs, the mind. Something as simple as elongating your breath, counting your breath or simply watching your breath creates huge benefits, not only intuitively but emotionally and physically.

When we begin to draw in the elements as we start to use them in our practices, we also start to connect our intuition to the power of life outside ourselves, helping to heighten our connection with the universe. We will use these elements to support our next exercises, to deepen our practice and our flow, and to expand our sacred space. We will also explore in the later pages of this book how to work with crystals or how to ground ourselves to tap into the earth elements, using a candle flame to aid in our manifestation or creation process and also as a tool for focus—tapping into our inner fire, using water to bathe and soothe the body and our emotions and, of course, breath work to tap into our inner and outer knowing. Using all these elements you will come to a deepened sense of knowing in your own circle of life.

Tapping into
the power of
breath makes an
unconditional
space within
the body.

# FINDING YOUR ELEMENTAL SYMBOLS

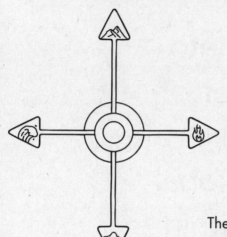

The four essential elements in the scheme of life—earth, air, fire and water—are elements that come together to form completion and wholeness in all living beings. Earth holds us, nourishes us; air gives our life movement and lift; fire is purest creation, power and passion; water drives our emotions and makes up a huge chunk of our physical being . . .

Let's look at the circle of growth in a plant—the soil (the earth) is the womb to the seed, the water nourishes the plant, the sun—that great ball of fire—feeds the plant, giving it the power of life to break through the earth and instinctively grow up toward the light (just like us!) and then the air carries the next seed to fertile land while the plant also cleanses our air. That plant then feeds the animals, feeds us and feeds the earth when it dies by fertilizing the land and becoming earth once more . . . cycle upon cycle affecting every moment of all our lives, so it's safe to say these are important elements and super-important cycles. The connective force, the cycle of connectivity between these elements is represented by a circle or wheel, so what better way to create and support a deeper sense of nourishing the self than by bringing these elements into your sacred space to represent the wholeness of life? You can acknowledge and then feel those properties begin to hold and harness you, as you strengthen your connection with intuition and as you work to manifest your hopes, dreams and desires, and heal your fears.

A beautifully simple way to pick the talismans to bring into your space that represent these four elements is to read aloud the descriptions below and allow your intuition to bring your mind's eye and your inner child together to daydream and show you what they look or feel like to you.

- **Earth** Nourishment, fertility, enrichment, infinite, creativity and longevity
- **Fire** Creativity, change, passion, power, potential and raw emotion
- **Water** Emotions, renewal, regeneration, purification and calm
- **Air** The breath of life, your voice, your spirit, freedom and flight

You could choose:

- A plant to represent earth, water and air.
- A crystal whose vibrations represent all the elements. You can go one step further by creating crystal grids or shapes with powerful formations.
- For earth, dried lavender, rose petals or Himalayan salts to represent the richness of the earth.
- For water, I tend to take a glass with me and drink it in as I sit and work with intuition, tapping deeper into spiritual, universal energy, but occasionally I add cut flowers that

THE LIFE-CHANGING POWER OF INTUITION

I've been gifted to represent this powerful energy and force.

- For air, I use my greatest vessels, my lungs, and I often support that by using incense sticks/cones or essential oil as it stimulates and relaxes the lungs and respiratory system, allowing me to deepen my breath capacity and also indulge in a scent that is relaxing and feels good.
- For fire, I strike a match as I arrive in the space to bring it all together and light a candle to create life.

These are just suggestions because this is a very personal practice. Ask yourself and your intuition what comes to life for you? How are these elements best represented for you? Take a breath, close your eyes if you need to, and let your answers be born intuitively and come to life from within you.

## OTHER ELEMENTAL REPRESENTATIONS

There is one more beautiful element to add to your sacred space and that is the element of spirit, the universe,

the higher knowing, being and its energy. As you create a scared space, as you place the talisman of each element in your space, you are not only drawing in the power, the energy and the vibration of each element, you are bringing together an energy of completeness, wholeness. Place them in a circle to heighten their meaning, one that allows us to bring in heaven to Earth—a space that allows you to sit within it so you become the conduit, the vessel, the embodiment of and for spirit. You are awakening a unique vibration and energy and will then be able to communicate with your intuition, your spirit and the universe, on a whole new level.

## LAYING OUT YOUR ENERGY/ TALISMAN CIRCLE

It's important that you keep your energy circle within your sacred space. I have my energy circle on a tabletop in my sacred space much like an altar and I've also had it on the floor and on a bookcase. I have a client who cleverly lays theirs out in a cupboard and another who keeps theirs in a beautiful wooden case that they take with them when they travel.

How you lay out your space, how you create your space or stage your altar is down to you and your intuition—use the circle formation as a starting point but remember it doesn't need to be perfect or exact. Create your space with the help of your intuition and use your senses to explore how a talisman feels when you place it—do you like or dislike where it is? Remember intuition uses all the senses to communicate your "YES" and your "NO," just as it does when moving furniture or placing a picture in your bedroom or living room—use what you have already learned, play with it—have fun!!

3

·

# EXPANDING YOUR PRACTICE

·

We have now connected to your intuition and developed a safe space for you to come to listen, learn and ask of it. This part of the book is where we will deepen your practices, pulling back the layers of the ego and fear. We'll work toward using your intuition in the key areas of life, with specific exercises for each, whether it's a bright sunny (literally and emotionally) day or one when the rain just won't stop pouring down.

To make intuition an everyday strength or even a superpower, we need to work it. "Finding Your Tells" (see page 53) is a powerful tool (and please keep the practice up), but we can also dive much deeper and expand much further your trust in your intuition and yourself. We can do so by healing those areas of life that have discouraged you from leaning into its call and by dissolving the fear and dialing down the ego. The potential of your intuitive muscles is extensive, but currently some intuitive calls and senses might feel as if they are dancing their own dance, flowing at their own rate and therefore jumping up and scaring you into action at random times of your life. We need to condition them to fire up and come together so that you can call upon it in times of need.

Some exercises may appear obvious. Good! That's what intuition does. It strips it all back and simplifies the "things" of life (decisions at work/in life, your attitude and energy, the ease at which you lean into living . . . anything and everything!) so that they start to feel obvious, but what often happens then is that your mind starts to kick in and complicates matters.

And then on the other hand, some of these exercises may feel somewhat obscure to you. Again, good! Let intuition take you out of your comfort zone and beautifully into its zone—all I ask is that you don't write it off before you've given it a go.

# For Everyday Intuition

As you work on your intuition, these teachings will evolve. The greater you trust in your skill and the more you do and the more you apply, the more you will allow intuition to become part of your every day and the more you'll instinctively trust it.

For a long time, I just considered that intuition found me in my meditation spot or in my sacred space, but that was just more fear, my ego saying that I am not good enough to use it out in the real world, that people would think me "strange." A huge part of my learning in life was about being brave and comfortable in who I am, and the more I embraced intuition in my every day, the more it became my norm every day, rather than my guilty little secret. My ego taught me through fear that I would be rejected for these beliefs but intuition just showed me, took me closer to those more open-minded folk or those ready to be more open to it and trusting in it.

So it's time to take the stabilizers off and pop your L plates in the bin once and for all. Let's build on your intuitive tells and add to and expand your body's responses to your intuitive calls. The feelings we are going to be activating here are tells that we can use in every everyday environments and that is super-important—often we can get so lost in the conversation that we forget to listen in to what intuition is telling us when it comes to asking, "Are these my people?," "Would it be good for me to go out to that bar tonight?," "What do they REALLY mean in that text . . . ?"

So much of our energy is spent on the people and the places we interact with and intuition is the protector of our energy, so let's look first at using our intuition to investigate who or what fulfills us, fuels and fires us up.

## WHO/WHAT IS AN ENERGY RADIATOR?

An energy radiator is someone or something, even some place, that radiates warmth and joy and brings comfort into your life just by you being in their/its presence. Like a radiator in your home, it heats you up, makes you feel safe, comfortable and warm. It can be a person or place, food or drink—anything that we interact with emotionally, physically or energetically. The energy, the warmth of these radiators can also be invoked when you bring them to mind (literally it's just like magic!), like a friend that makes you feel super-good and upbeat or a holiday destination that warms you just by taking your memory there. A text or an email from such a person will carry with it an intention of bringing you love and warmth—it will fill you with the essence of GOOD.

## INTUITIVE TELL:

Our intuition likes to give us tells within our body that feel playful, that are quite literal and that make sense to us. Our tells for this particular ask tend to radiate from the body, so you are likely to find your tell for the radiators in your life in a body sensation, a prickle, pulse, heat or cool breeze most likely in your arms, your legs, your fingers or toes.

## WHAT OR WHO IS MY ENERGY DRAIN?

A drain is someone or something that depletes our energy or leaves our mind feeling tired, heavy or sad, knowingly or unknowingly. It can be someone or some place whose vibration or values feel off-key to your own. Just like you, their energy will change depending on their situation so just because their vibe or intention is set to drain you today, it doesn't mean it will tomorrow, but only intuition, not ego, can tell you that. A text or an email from such a person will leave you feeling as though you want to ignore it or make your eye roll—check in with that.

### INTUITIVE TELL:

Intuition again is smart. To alert you to a place, person or space that pulls you down or depletes you, it tends to use your body spaces that have circular openings or entry points—places that energy could pour out from (if you close your eyes and use your imagination) and also those parts of your body that are designed to move energy away from you—so we're talking your ears, nose, mouth, eyes and your belly button!

The next tells are more emotional and energetical. Once developed they can be used to dive deeper when investigating your relationships and places of work.

## IS IT "MINE"?

This is perhaps the most important of all your tells. It is much more interpersonal, much more in the emotional realm—often we can walk into a room and feel an energetical weight or sense someone is annoyed and we automatically assume that heavy feeling, that heavy emotion, is ours or is because of us. It's absolutely crucial that we stop assuming that all things hard and heavy must be ours to deal with. When you walk into that room and feel a sadness, you can focus back within yourself, transport yourself back to your sacred space to connect with your intuition and ask, "Is this mine?" and then wait for intuition's response to guide you. It will advise you whether the sadness is your own (so you can go safely and look deeper) or if it's someone else's (so you can send it love rather than harbor it yourself).

## INTUITIVE TELL:

This will be a feeling that comes from within. It could be a warming pulse, coolness at your heart or your belly or a rising feeling throughout your body. Don't overlook sensations at your heart, at your throat or around your mind's eye/your forehead.

## IS IT SOMEONE ELSE'S?

If you dive into a space and it feels "off" and it's not yours, it's important to have an opposing tell to "Is it mine?" so that you have confirmation that your intuitive feelings are spot on. When that tell signals to you, it's important that you stay grounded and centered in yourself—all energy is very powerful but it requires an invitation into our body and our psyche. See the cleansing instructions on page 106 if you feel or sense (or are shown intuitively) that you are holding on to a suitcase full of energy and emotion that is not yours to carry.

## INTUITIVE TELL:

Energy when it is not our own feels heavy (we will explore that in the next chapter) and it can leave us with a headache (hence the need to cleanse and ground). If the energy/emotion belongs to someone else, your intuition is likely to develop your tell as a feeling of a weight lifting away or onto your shoulders, from your back or the back of your neck.

## WHAT'S MY RADIATOR, WHAT'S MY DRAIN?
## IS IT MINE, IS IT SOMEONE ELSE'S?

We now need to locate and train your unique intuitive tells so that they will be ready to take into real-life situations.

Firstly, you will need to warm them up by using them in louder and larger spaces—it may sound counter-intuitive but the more intimate the situation, the more personal, the harder it can feel to catch and trust our intuition as we feel under the spotlight of another gaze.

When there is more going on around you, you can use that to give you time to step back from center stage and dial in to your intuition and not feel so much pressure to join in or draw awareness to the fact you are slightly outside of what is going on. Otherwise it can feel like you are having two conversations at once, one with friends and family and one with intuition; to start with that can feel like you are being pulled in each direction and also overwhelming—so step back. If you are one-on-one with another, it's much harder to keep a conversation going and check in with intuition at the same time, though in time you will be spinning the conversation and picking up with your intuition as if it was second nature.

Always practice these exercises first in your sacred space so that you can lean on its protection and trust with more clarity in its voice when you take it out into the world! Remember— always cleanse and ground yourself before and after practice or when out on the world's stage (see pages 106 and 210).

Listen to your inner voice, see with your third eye, feel with your gut.

# FEELING THE TELLS

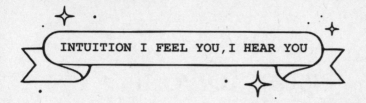

INTUITION I FEEL YOU, I HEAR YOU

For this particular exercise, I recommend sitting on a chair because it's important to feel your feet on the ground and that your spine is supported because your intuition can appear in your limbs—my "What's my radiator?" comes running down my left leg and especially in my knee and my "Who is my drain?" sounds like a fuzzy white noise in my left ear and when I first felt that I felt a little wobbly afterward!

I like to do this next part with music and specifically music without lyrics because words can distract us, whereas the vibration of the music allows us to sink deeper within and become more alert to the tells that intuition is drawing us toward. (I suggest "Islands" by Ludovico Einaudi, but there are more recommendations in further reading on page 243.) We use music in our practice here because out in the real world it's important to be able to tune out life's noise and conversation, so ego doesn't trick you into distraction.

As with any of these practices you can read the guide out loud or record yourself reading the steps, so you can play back and listen to yourself as an audio guide. In time, you won't need to follow the steps to connect.

## 1/

Sitting comfortably, eyes open—this is important as it will be hard for you to tune in with your eyes closed for long periods of time in a meeting or at a party.

## 2/

Feeling your feet against the ground, against the floor, shift your weight a little into your heels, then wriggle your toes before planting them down firmly into the ground—find the balance between heel and toes, centered, grounded.

## 3/

As you turn to your breath, begin to feel the weight of your feet, sink into the ground beneath you, turn your palms face up, ready and open to receive (an indicator to the universe and spirit) and lay them comfortably on your knees. Wriggle the fingers a little and then allow them to settle.

## 4/

Come to your breath: in through the nose, out through the mouth. Breathe in for a count of six, exhale for a count of seven, out through an open mouth. Repeat this cycle seven times—a now-familiar signal to your intuition that you are here and ready to connect. After the cycle of seven, breathe in and out through your nose and mouth, allow your breath to steady and become natural and neutral.

We now call your intuition in your sacred space. Do this out loud (that's my favorite) or ask in your mind or from the heart (whatever feels best to you): "Intuition I feel you, I hear you, I allow you" and repeat this call three times. Allow yourself to surrender, feel the energy of the room and your space holding you safe and steady, swirling lovingly around as you feel it intensify and become more apparent. This will help you prepare to connect, and with each time you call and each practice you take, it will get quicker and easier—just like a second breath in your body.

5/
With eyes still open, start to visualize a circle of light or of color (however is right or however is shown to you) at your mind's eye—that circle may project itself outside your body or it may be shown or felt to you in your belly, your solar plexus. If you feel you are struggling, repeat, "I surrender and I allow. I am and I can." Within that circle now is a dial—for some this is a clock, for

others a compass—let it tell you its own truth. As you connect, intuition begins to move the dial, spinning it clockwise or anticlockwise (your intuition will choose). It will spin fast at first, then come to settle—this is how you know you are connected deeply.

Now we very simply ask your intuition to connect with your tells for:

TELL ONE:
THE ENERGY RADIATORS

Focusing on the dial, ask out loud or again in mind: "Intuition you see me, you know me, I now trust that you hold me. Please show me in my limbs, in the extensive parts of my body, what my signal is when you sense an energy radiator before me."
　　Repeat this five times.
　　Now close your eyes, you sink deeper without effort and allow yourself to feel your intuition in your body—watch how the tell shows within your body. Trust what your intuition is saying to you, how it is showing to you—accept it and remember it. Most importantly, write it down in a notebook—let's log it all!

## TELL TWO:
### THE ENERGY DRAINS

Now it's time for the next ask.

With your eyes open come back to visualizing, sensing your circle (however it is shown or felt to you) and its intuitive dial—breathe, watch and allow as the dial spins, as you connect with your intuition once more. Don't pressure yourself for it and if you feel stuck or are leaning into frustration, repeat "I surrender and I allow." When you feel ready (remember there is never any rush) ask in your mind or out loud, "Dear intuition, you guide me so sweetly and I have come to know and accept that not all energy is good nor right for me. Please may I ask that you show here my tell within my body, my being." Repeat this five times.

Close your eyes now and feel it. Trust it, accept it, remember it, then write that down too.

## TELL THREE:
### IS IT MINE?

Now we move on to the next tell, but do not rush through all of these tell connections—take a break, you can always tune back in via the first six steps, via the breath, via the dial, whenever you need.

Again, with your eyes open, we come to the breath, to visualize and feel for your circle, your dial as before—allow it to spin at its own rate, no pressure on you nor it. Remember that this is a much more personal sensation—it's a feeling that intuition will rise through your body and so we need to be very aware of all sensations in our body as we ask our intuition: "To myself, I know; to myself, be true. Guide me and help me sense and feel my tell that signals that which I should be leaning into." Repeat seven times—we need a little more time here as this intuitive feeling comes from a deep space within and can often feel a little more like a ghost when it starts to show itself— have patience, keep the breath, keep the faith that gives it strength.

When you are ready, close your eyes and allow yourself to feel that warmth or coolness that is rising in or blowing through the body. Trust it, accept it, remember it—and write it down.

## TELL FOUR:
### IS IT SOMEONE ELSE'S?

We come back now once again with your eyes open, to feel for and visualize our circle and our dial—yes you have got this! We come to the breath as we connect with our intuition and surrender to watching that now familiar dial spin once again and deepen our connection with intuition. When you are ready, and always take your own time, ask your intuition: "I need to ask is this mine or is this theirs? Please show me when the energy is proving too much and weighing heavy like a chore. Whose it is that I should be looking out for?" Again, we repeat this seven times as this is a much more inter-personal tell so it can take a little longer to show.

Come to close your eyes now and allow yourself to feel for intuition, for your tell—remember when an energy, mood or an emotion belongs to someone else. Your intuition is likely to develop your tell as a feeling of a weight lifting away or onto your shoulders, from your back or the back of your neck. Trust it, accept it, remember it—and write it down.

After you have connected with intuition, whether you do a tell a day or you do them all at once, ground yourself (you will find exercises and ways to ground on page 210). Get back into the body, back into the here and now and the everyday. As much as we would love to float out in this space all day, the importance of this work is that we ground it back to earth.

# FEELING THE TELLS
## at a glance

**Sit comfortably** with your eyes open.

**Feel your feet** against the floor before planting them down firmly into the ground.

**Gently close your eyes** and turn your palms face up, open to receiving.

**Come to your breath:** in through your nose, out through the mouth. Breathe in for a count of six, exhale for a count of seven. Repeat this cycle seven times.

**Now call your intuition in** to your sacred space. Either out loud or in your mind ask, "Intuition I feel you, I hear you" and repeat this call three times.

**Allow yourself to surrender,** feel the energy of the room and your space holding you safe and steady.

**Open your eyes** and start to visualize a circle of light or color in your mind's eye. This circle may project itself outside your body or it may be felt in your belly. If you feel you are struggling, repeat, "I surrender and I allow. I am and I can."

**Envision a dial within the circle**. As you connect, intuition beings to move the dial, spinning it clockwise or anticlockwise (your intuition will choose). It will spin fast at first, then come to settle.

**Now very simply ask** your intuition to connect with your tells.

# Taking Your Intuitive Tells
# Out on to the Road

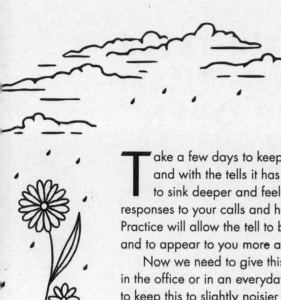

Take a few days to keep checking in with your intuition and with the tells it has given you—this will allow you to sink deeper and feel the consistency of intuition's responses to your calls and how that feels now in your body. Practice will allow the tell to become clearer and stronger, and to appear to you more and more quickly . . .

Now we need to give this a real-life test. This can be in the office or in an everyday social situation—remember to keep this to slightly noisier situations, so you can practice leaning into intuition without looking like you are leaning out of your friends' conversation. While your trust is developing, I advise you to avoid a pub or bar (or any other environment that involves alcohol) to actively road-test this—because this can open us up to other emotional and energetical layers and can crowd into our ego and become a mega distraction.

# USING YOUR TELLS AND TAKING THEM OUT IN THE OPEN

Before you leave home,
it's good to use your practice
to gauge how the day ahead
looks and feels for you.

Remember intuition has the power to connect to the universe and therefore with the energy that awaits you, so we will go to your sacred space and intuitively ask quite literally how the day is looking—think of it like checking the weather forecast. Again, the response from intuition will become quicker over time and you can tweak your ask as you so need.

Come to the breath—those seven delicious arriving breaths—in through the nose out through the mouth—come to visualize, sense and allow your connecting circle or your dial to come to mind or extend beyond you. As you connect deeper to intuition, allow the dial to move, then come to ask whatever is on your mind today—close your eyes and say it out loud or in your mind, for example:

"What will work be like today?" Ask three times—listen, look and feel for how intuition tickles your radiator or drain tell in answer to this question. Listen and allow yourself to feel and hear.

If you feel the warmth of an energy radiator, you can bounce out the house. If you feel a drain, do not worry! Your intuition is simply letting you know so that you can remain mindful and gently vigilant of where the drain might be coming from—a

person, perhaps, or is it a sign that you are sitting too long at your screen? Remember intuitive work is healing and is meant to help us take control of things that we may have been unaware of and that haven't been so great for us.

Now you are ready to take this out of your home.

As you step into your office, for example, plant your feet on the floor as we did back in our connecting exercise (see page 78), take a breath, keep your eyes open and allow yourself to connect, to sense and to see your circle, the spinning dial. Feel how safe you are, how protected; when you are ready, you can ask intuition for insight into the mood in the room, "How is the energy in the room right now?" Look for radiators and drain tells and then ask "Is it mine, is it someone else's?" Let your intuition respond—trust it, don't force it. Remember too that intuition only knows love and kindness so it will guide you to where you are best placed today— maybe you sit where you always sit, maybe you find a different seat for today around different people or maybe it alerts you to take your whole lunch break and get outdoors as you have become drained by technology or the hard work you are pouring yourself into. Keep the conversation with your intuition alive—it doesn't just wait for you at home, it is you and so it's with you at all times!

Other ways I have come to be thankful for intuition's hand-holding is in a meeting or in a one-on-one or even a date. Connect in as you now know how—feet grounded, allow your circle and the dial to spin, and ask and listen for its response. Watch how it develops over the day or week. Again, do not back away from your colleague if your tell indicates they are a drain—remember we've all got a lot going on and our energy changes over the day. Remember this is also an opportunity to learn—to consider how all our energy, yours included, has an effect on all those we come into contact with. Be mindful of how you need to be responsible for your own energy, so that you can safely be around someone whose energy is draining you—you can't always pick your teammates, but you can use intuition to uncover how best you can be around them or how to move away or take loving space from them for the highest good of yourself.

When you are choosing your lunch, ask your intuition "Is this good for me, will it give me the energy I need?" (Is it a drain or a radiator?) If you are choosing a snack, don't be surprised if your intuition gives chocolate a thumbs-up! Chocolate too can be good on the right occasions!

When you come home, seek some intuitive self-care or general cleansing (see page 106). When we come to read the energy of a space or of other people, it's important that we cleanse this energy, together with any baggage from the day, from our being, ESPECIALLY if you are concerned that you are becoming overloaded with another's "stuff."

Sometimes you may feel that you are reading it inaccurately or getting it wrong. You may feel that you are not as good or as confident when you take this out of the sacred space. That's OK—you are learning and there's a whole section later in the book to help you to combat the fear and the doubt. Remember, in getting it "wrong," you are really learning just how to get it right.

## INTUITION ONLINE

Now let's come to the place where the ego and your fear can really draw their energy—the online world. Practice with work emails to start with as they tend to be more measured, more thought through than text messages.

As always, we come back to the breath, to the circle and to the dial—this process will now be becoming more and more like a second breath to you with every tune-in.

Here are some questions for your intuition to help you navigate the online forums:

- "What is their energetical intention toward me? Is it from their heart or from their ego?"
- "Can I trust this?"
- "Should I follow them?"
- "Are they saying what they truly mean?"
- "Is this for real or is this for show?"
- "Do they like me for the right reasons?"
- "Do I really like or need this?"
- "Are they being good toward me?"
- "Do they/does this want to build me up or tear me down?"

These are a guide for your intuitive work but you can shape them with your own voice. You just need to be clear and to ask your intuition directly. Don't fear intuition's reaction—it will never tell you off nor punish you. Its purpose is to guide you to what is best for you, but if you feel you have to move away from its direction, that's OK because there is learning here too—if we don't know what getting it wrong feels like, if we didn't know how going against what is really good for us felt like, we wouldn't be learning.

Over time the bond with your intuition will strengthen and you won't have to use your human voice to ask your intuition. The bond will become powerful and the ask subconscious—it will feel as if your intuition is reading your mind, stepping in before you even need to ask it a question. Practice will make you a better listener and will give your intuition more power and clarity.

And on the days that you do "get it wrong," don't give up—intuition never ever gives up on you so please don't give up on yourself. You just need to spend more time in your safe space, going back through your tell exercises, reconnecting to yourself, your intuition, your power.

Over time the bond
with your intuition
will strengthen.

# The Power Within You: Your Energy, the Universe and You

You are more powerful than you can even imagine or will ever really know. We tend to condition ourselves into accepting what is given to us, believing that what we get is what we deserve and not asking for more just because, well why should we? Every so often though we have sweet moments of rebellion when our brain feels as if it might implode with one more crushing, self-annihilating thought, where we feel a fire in our belly or a kick in our gut.

It's a cycle we need to break or even to unlearn. Start to consider that instead of us being average human beings, we are all hyper-intelligent forces, with our own unique scale and with the potential to connect to a great force.

So let's look at the energy of our beautiful being.

## OUR ENERGY NETWORK

Our energy network is made up of chakras or energy centers—name it how you will! Think about how the leaves of trees use photosynthesis to draw energy from the sun, air and ground and then transfer it into food for its growth and nourishment. Our chakras or energy centers are like leaves. They are openings or entry points for the universal energy or life force to connect and flow into our own energy network. Each chakra has a unique purpose and power that allows us to connect to and then draw in the "light" from the universal life force; they also allow us to release gently back to the universe that which energetically or emotionally no longer serves us well.

So why do we need to know about our energy when we investigate our intuition? Our intuition communicates and travels through our body along this network, so it's super-important that we keep these channels open and connected.

We each also have an aura or field of energy that is emitted around our body with our own unique vibrational quality—our aura is made up of vibes and these vibes have a frequency that reflects the emotions and physical status of our human and emotional body. It is how we connect to another's energy, to spirit, to the universe and beyond. It is through our aura that we really first meet each other—our energy introduces us before we speak because it touches people before our words do—and it can be affected by our mood or situation.

It's also how our intuition reaches beyond ourselves in order to read danger or joy—it reaches out and touches the energy in a room, of a situation or of other people. Always remember that intuition works through love, never fear, so please don't be afraid of it—that's just ego waving its hand and trying to regain control over you once again. Intuition is there to help you keep moving forward, striding ahead confidently or redirecting if and when necessary.

When we keep our energy centers aligned, clear and cleansed, we create balance and harmony in our mind, body and spirit and intuition and your energy can connect with others on "your vibe" and draw them nearer toward you. When you are balanced and aligned your body becomes a super vessel—for energy flows clearer and with greater intention and potency, your energy reaches wider and as such intuition can move toward spirit and the universe (or whatever that is for you), to seek guidance for your highest good and communicate that with more clarity through the super antenna that is your body. You can also work with intuition in this state to plant the seeds of your heart's desires and work toward manifesting a greater future. From here we can also start to understand and teach ourselves our life's true purpose and power.

So, let's get to work. Decide whether you would like to record yourself reading the meditation to use as a guide or to read it out loud. Don't feel any pressure to know it off by heart—in time, you will intuitively know which step follows next!

●

# Always remember that intuition works through love, never fear.

●

# THE CHAKRA CLEANSE AND CONNECTION MEDITATION

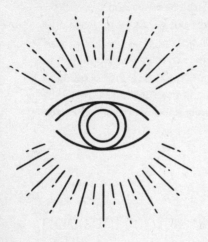

Really, really, really focus on surrendering into this mediation. Because connecting with your intuitive power means heightening a connection with your own personal energy universe and vice versa. As you expand your universe, you effortlessly expand your intuitive feelings and "seeings."

1/

Lie on your bed, or better yet the floor. It's also fine to sit upright depending on how you are feeling today, both emotionally and physically. Feel the weight of your body against the floor and turn your attention inward, closing your eyes when or if you so wish (if you are not reading this to yourself as a story!).

2/

Come to your mind's eye, your third eye, take a cleansing breath in through your nose and visualize that breath firing through the mind's eye. Repeat this gently three times.

3/

Using your breath, scan your body for any tension, knots or build-up in the mind from the day—take your awareness to your feet, your heels, your toes—as you breathe in, your awareness moves all the way up your body to your crown and the top of your head. With every breath you release any tension and it falls away without force or effort. The weight of your mood or any emotions from the day will gently start to lift as your body melts back down beneath

you and your breath continues to lengthen. However you feel, surrender and allow it.

4/

Start to visualize roots now growing out from the back of your head and neck, all along the spine, the backs of your arms, legs and then feet. These roots grow down deep into the ground beneath you and with every breath they are moving deeper and deeper down toward the earth's core. You are now planted, rooted and connected to the earth. She is holding you ready for greater sensory travel.

5/

Feel a cool breeze now beginning to move over your body. This may feel strange at first but it will quickly shift to feel more comfortable and soothing.

6/

Come deeper within, to your first energy center, the base chakra. Focus your intention and intuition there by visualizing or sensing a red light that is pulsing like a beacon at the point where your bottom touches the floor. Send your breath down toward your base and allow and sense the light grow in intensity and clarity. Watch as your energy center opens wider with each breath and starts to spin like a Catherine wheel, powerful, yet not out of control. As your energy center opens, it lovingly and gently releases anything energetically or emotionally that may have been holding you back or that has become clogged with energy soot. Let your intuition flash a sign to you that you are clear, aligned and ready to move to the next energy center or chakra point—let what comes to mind energetically come and go as it needs, affirming, "I am, I am, I am" three times over—without fear or judgment.

## 7/

Breathe in now and pull your intention and breath up into your sacrum, that space just above your pubis: this is your second energy center. Watch now as an orange light pulses here in recognition of you. Take your intuition there on the breath—watch as it cleanses and clears this center, releasing any unneeded emotion or worn feelings. Watch the light spin as intuition delivers to you a sign that tells you

that you are flowing freely here now and affirm, "I feel, I feel, I feel." Repeat three times.

## 8/

Climbing up your body with your breath once again, we move to your solar plexus or third energy center— your personal power center right at your belly. Watch or sense a yellow ball of light, like that of the sun, deepening in intensity and widening in scale with each and every breath. Feel a smile take over your face as you connect to your power, allowing your intuition to cleanse and clear any energy that has held you back or blocked you from feeling the true nature of your personal power. When your intuition signals to you that it's time to move on, accept it and affirm, "I can I can I can." Repeat three times.

## 9/

Now we move to the heart center, your fourth energy center, located in the center of your breastbone. Take your intuition there on your breath, watch or sense a green light spinning powerfully yet calmly, growing and widening with the power and clarity of your hopes and desires. With each breath, you are releasing fears and worn ideals; let them come, let them go and await your intuition's instruction that it's time to move up once more as you affirm, "I love, I love, I love." Repeat three times.

10/

Come now to see a blue light gently calling you at your throat chakra, which is your fifth energy center, located as per its namesake. We hold so much tension here, from old words spoken or held in anger toward yourself or another, so with every breath, surrender to forgiveness and with every breath of forgiveness watch as this blue light deepens and shifts in color and intensity. Once again, wait once more for your intuition to tell you to move upward as you affirm, "I speak, I speak, I speak." Repeat three times.

11/

As we move into our mind's eye or third eye, which is your sixth chakra, allow a darkness first to wash through your eyes. Let it be, don't fear it. A pinpoint of violet/purple light will pierce through the darkness, opening what looks and feels like a heavy safety curtain covering the stage of

a theater. With every breath, you open this dark curtain to reveal a purple light embodying the shape of you. You are there, standing with arms open wide on the stage—your stage. Watch yourself and smile at the connection as intuition uses your breath to cleanse and clear the stage. Wait until the illuminated purple-lit version of yourself looks up to the heavens as intuition then powers up and moves through into the crown center located at the top of your head, the energy doorway that connects you to your spiritual and universal understanding and knowing. The violet purple light of your third eye opens up into a deep, velvet purple light—allow yourself to bathe in this light and with every breath, rise up and beyond, away from your body, gently float and lift. As you lift here affirm "I see, I see, I see," repeating three times.

12/

As you continue to move sky high, you sense a creamy white light pulsing like a flashlight or a twinkling star in the night's sky—send your intuition there on your breath. Watch as that white light opens out toward you like a beautiful lily. With every breath, watch as that light of your energy center spins up and through your crown to connect with this beautiful white light—this is the light of the universe, of spirit. Sense the skies above you and feel that you and that light could go on forever. Watch as your energy spirals together with this universal force, watch and feel how they intertwine effortlessly, how they are effortlessly connected. Affirm, "I am more than I know, the universe and spirit fuels me, feeds me and I trust in its support and willingly follow its intuitive guidance and flow." Repeat three times.

## 13/

Feel your intuition fly up to this point of connection, watch as it draws the light from this great power, this energy and life force down through your crown, through your mind's eye or third eye, down through the throat, through the heart, through the solar plexus, the sacrum right down to the base and down into Mother Earth. Allow yourself to feel that light charge though your body, moving up and down, gentle yet powerful, pouring more and more light into each chakra. Feel that energy now holding hands with your intuition as

they expand and radiate outward from your body and being. Allow yourself to see your aura—your own energy field.

## 14/

Feel yourself energetically floating or swimming through this fantastic light display as you come to realize that your intuition has taken you energetically beyond your body and through the mind's eye or third eye. Sense how you are able to move or float up through your energy field and explore it safely with your intuition.

## 15/

Watch and feel the vivid colors spin and blend together as you turn back to witness the beauty of your human body. Notice the energy centers— your chakra points. These great lights are pulsing in unison, balanced, happy and healthy, radiating up toward you and up toward that greater power.

## 16/

Turn your mind's eye up now toward the stars in the sky. Allow yourself to feel how wonderous you truly are and how safe it feels to expand out into every extension of your being. Feel safe and secure in the limitlessness of your nature. Feel your roots and energy centers supporting you there. Watch and listen for any of your tells, any visions you see or sense, acknowledge them, yet do not tether them.

## 17/

Allow your intuition to take you now for five minutes (maybe longer!) wherever it wants you to "see and feel." Affirm, "I remember I remember I remember" (repeat three times) and when you return you will remember your travels and what intuition and that great energy want to teach you today. If you are reading this as a guide, close your eyes now, sink back deeper and let go—you are safe in Intuition's hands.

## 18/

When you are ready to return, you will feel or see yourself gently floating back into your body, you will just feel very awake. You will start to become more aware of your breath and the shape and weight of your body. See the light from your energy centers and feel your chakras spinning in harmony as that cool breeze returns now, moving over you like a duvet,

sealing in these good feelings, protecting you, sealed in your light.

## 19/

Scan your body, up from your toes, from your feet, up along your body, right up to the top of your head once more and affirm, "I am totally safe, I am totally protected"(repeat three times). Take three cleansing breaths in through the nose and out through the mouth as your awareness returns back to your body and rises up into the room and, when you are ready, open your eyes.

CARE INSTRUCTIONS: Take time to get up slowly after this exercise and drink plenty of water. If you are feeling a little light-headed, turn to the grounding exercise on page 210.

## EXPANDING THIS PRACTICE

You can use the chakra cleanse and connection meditation for a specific chakra or energy center if you feel tension there or when you want to boost its power or send light there. For example, when we have an argument we can feel tense in the throat and tummy, this is because our chakras have retreated or "shrunk in" as your body seeks to protect you, so using the chakra meditation will reawaken your intuition, reconnect with the universal life force and use its soothing energy to heal.

body. Using your breath, allow your intuition to draw the crystal's energy and healing force in through the chakras, the energy centers in the palms of your hands as you work through the meditation above or just while you move yourself to sleep at night. We can also use color here—the color of the crystal that reflects the color of the light we draw into each energy center will also help you to drive the healing energy via your intuition and your intent to where it needs to be.

## CRYSTALS

I also recommend incorporating crystals, whose energy vibration correspond to each chakra in your practice. You can lay each on its associated chakra during the meditation or you can also use a crystal to heighten the vibration and power of each center throughout the day. Hold the appropriate crystal in your hands or lay it along the

Chuck it in
the fuck-it
bucket and
move on.

# Cleansing
# Your Energy

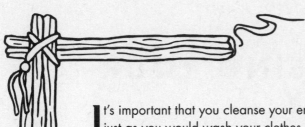

It's important that you cleanse your energy to keep it fresh just as you would wash your clothes, body or your hair because energy clings and lingers and over time it can become dense and a heavy load to carry. To cleanse energy that has stagnated over time or to cleanse from harsh words or difficult situations, we turn to nature and the elements.

Water is great for rinsing away emotional heaviness or soaking it off in the bath and I have provided some bath soaks for you (see pages 198–207). The shower is a powerful tool and will wash your body from the crown down the body through the energy centers right down and out to the feet. I like to visualize all the negative energy swilling down the plughole.

For air, I come always to the breath. I count the breath, carry out a guided meditation or I head for a walk or a run, moving through the air so it can move through me.

For fire, I use nature's scents as my tools—white sage and palo santo (the sacred wood from a tree that grows in South America) are two of my favorites. I use white sage after every energy session, especially after heavier energy work. Never underestimate the power of a hug or how intuitively your energy goes to shield and protect those who seem more vulnerable than you, but like a sponge you cannot help but soak up some of that toxicity.

Sweet-smelling palo santo feels lighter to me and I tend to use this as a cleansing tool for the everyday. I recommend using it when you get home from work or when you need a little pick-me-up or energy refresh.

# CLEANSING YOUR ENERGY

Carry out this practice standing up please. We can move energy out of our being, deep into the ground and into Mother Nature, just by placing our feet on the ground and feeling the magnetic draw of the power of you connecting to the power of the earth and her energy field.

Think of cleansing your intuitive body just as you would dust the rooms of your house—you have to get into the corners and blast not just the dust you can see but also the dust bunnies hidden behind the doors.

Set light to the sage leaves, smudge stick or palo santo wood with a match or candle and lightly blow on it to give more life to the smoke. The smoke is key here because the smoke is naturally drawn energetically to the spaces or places that are harboring the most negative Intent and this is where we brush or sweep away the energy that no longer serves us or that isn't ours to carry from our body.

## 1/

Standing in your sacred space, holding your chosen cleansing tool at least one hand's length away from your body at all times—PLEASE do not make contact with your skin—let the smoke cleanse you (but don't let the heat burn you!).

## 2/

Waft your tool back and forth between your legs. This cleanses the base chakra, where we hold most of other people's "stuff."

## 3/

Next waft your tool gently up along the chakra points, from the base to the sacrum, to the solar plexus, to the heart, then up to the throat. Repeat three times.

## 4/

Turn to the corners of your body, fanning the tool under your feet, behind your knees, under your armpits, in between your fingers and around the back of your neck.

## 5/

To release any feeling of people talking about you "behind your back," work the tool, brushing or sweeping it literally behind your back. Lightly fan your tool along your back or along your spine as best you can. You can ask someone you love to do this for you.

## 6/

Next lightly hold the tool a hand's distance away from your mind's eye or third eye in an act of cleaning your intentions—your sight and your lens on life. Keep your tool a safe distance from your eyes though!

## 7/

Finally draw the tool up to the crown and allow the smoke to carry any negative thoughts or restrictions up and away from you. Send them back to that great power in the universe.

## 8/

Take a moment to stand and just be. Take three long breaths in through the nose and out, sighing, through the mouth.

## 9/

Feel your feet once against the ground. Give your toes a wriggle and affirm with your heart and mind, "I am totally cleansed, totally safe, grounded and protected." You are now cleansed, your energy refreshed and ready to go.

As you cleanse yourself in your scared space, you should also cleanse the energies of the space! Follow the steps above but fan or waft your cleansing tool in and around your sacred space, especially in the corners, knowing that energy soot can linger here as dust does.

Intuition will never be your enemy—it's forever your loyal friend.

# Asking for Something Bigger

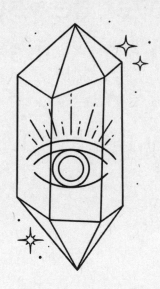

We can sit back in life and let it take us peacefully (as we will allow it!) along the road, letting things unwind and unfold in their own time. Or we can lean into and ask of life to help us make or deliver (with acceptance, surrender and practice) what or who is for our highest good—be that the job you dream of, the holiday or the love that feels good to and for you. More often than not though, we feel guilty for asking for more or we go to the other end of the spectrum and get angry when what we want doesn't arrive neatly wrapped on our doorstep, complete with a returns sticker if we decide we don't like it (that's your ego, by the way!).

With our intuition and a little human mapping we can tap into the energies of the universe to create, manifest and attract good wishes, good vibes and desires into your life, and into your being. I emphasize good here because these are born from the right place, from deep within you and created in the heart space, rather than hurriedly, in an ego-induced state of material want.

How do you identify the differences between what you want and what you think you want? The answer is to use our mind's eye, or third eye.

## MANIFESTATION AND INTENTION
## BOARDS AND LISTS

Have you been asked what would you wish for if you had three wishes? The minute I am asked, my brain goes blank and I can't even think of one thing. This is because wishes are not thought-led, but inspired by intuition.

When we set our sights on something or someone, we go out of our way to get it, don't we? Often these desires or wants are for short-lived excitement and it never really matches up to how you dreamed it would be. So then when someone asks you to "dream, ask and to believe," you are skeptical. You've been influenced by past experiences and disappointments. You think to yourself, "Why bother this time, when it didn't work out like I wanted last time . . . ?"

But that's the crux of it. It was about "wanting" something or someone, but we don't own or control these things and you will end up shrinking yourself to fit them or that, to get what you think you "want" instead of flying high on your own. So, when you start to craft, be aware that intuition always works on energy, not material goals. Many people miss the delights and blessings of a delivery from the universal energy because they have become fixated on how it "should" look and that it's not "exactly as I wanted," forgetting that intuition has created it from how it should feel for your good, and not your wants—remember 99.9999% of the time we are selling ourselves short with ego as a guide, aiming for a goal we think reachable—and it actually causes us to reach down, not up and in turn we feel down on ourselves, life and spirit.

Here are a few things you can practice. Choose which feels right for you. Some of us are more visual, some of us like to cut and paste with glue and paper, some are writers, others make lists—perhaps you've been told you are one not the other . . . don't write off what you think you are not. I was told at school that I was rubbish at writing (never one for staying in the margin me!) and look at me now . . . break the conditioning and let your intuition use these guides to move you into how it should really come to life for you. This is "visualization into actualisation."

Intuitive manifestation-building is not a rushed process, but equally don't allow yourself to slide into procrastination. To prevent this, ask your intuition to flag when you're approaching that slide. A clue might be when you put it off until "I'm better/stronger/not so busy/in the right place . . ." You can quickly tap into your intuition to check where you are really at, as you are now using it in your everyday it has become a strong muscle. Ask it, "Am I procrastinating?," "Should I start today?" or "Am I putting it off in fear and in doubt?" Feel for your "YES" and "NO" tells, and your radiator or your drain tells. You've got this.

# VISUALIZATION

Visualization is a powerful intuitive tool, but sometimes you don't know how "it's" going to look just yet, so you need to step into your sacred space for an intuitive daydream.

Take three categories: for example, love, work and health.

I recommend setting a timer on your phone (but put your phone in airplane mode to prevent distraction) and allow five minutes for each question you have to ask. Then light a candle and look deep into the flame—that signature element for pure creation and the spark of new beginnings. Place your hands on your heart and come toward intuition, use your breath to sink into its loving grip. Closing your eyes, turn your intention inward and ask of intuition and yourself to connect with your highest good as you say out loud or in your mind:

"What is my dream for love?" Repeat three times, let the breath fill you and let the intuitive daydream play out.

OR

"What is my dream, my goal for work?" Repeat three times and let the visualization play out, let it flow.

OR

"What is my dream for my health?" Repeat three times and let the daydream unfold.

Don't worry if nothing profound appears immediately, these things take a little practice, patience and time as you move beyond your "norm." You are opening a door to your intuitive dreams; these are not sleep dreams, they are messaging from your future self, spirit and intuition and they may not pop in immediately, so let the time flow, come to the breath and repeat, "I am and I can. I am seeing, I am feeling, I am and I can connect to intuition and we are feeling from the universe." When the timer sounds, write down everything you saw. Remember that ego limits what you see and disregards some features in our mind's eye as unimportant, so they may not pack a punch or make complete sense now, but may come to make sense weeks or months later.

## FLOW-WRITE WITH INTUITION

You can also write these questions out by hand and start making lists. You can do this wherever your flow catches you. Sometimes it speaks to me on the bus, so I write using my Notes app on my phone, unwilling to miss the wave. There is one rule—don't overthink it! Just write freely—no judgment here—and your intuition will take you to places you have never thought of. Make time in your sacred space to review your notes once a week (I do this on a Sunday with a cup of tea).

## AN INTUITIVE INTENT BOARD

Go visual—literally—and as big as you like. Get a sketch pad or a sheet of paper. Write your intuitive ask in the middle of the sheet and then gather images that resonate with your intuition. Find them anywhere you like—magazines or papers—and cut, stick and montage them on a board or in a book. Try not to be too literal with material asks (a picture of a car, for example), and add colors and textures, feelings and words. You can do this in one afternoon or you

can gather images over time. This is great to do with your kids, friends or partner—make it as social or as private as you wish.

If you are more comfortable with tech rather than pen and paper, start a Pinterest board (or a PowerPoint presentation or create a file on your desktop). Add to it for five minutes every day, such as when on a break from work (remember you are allowed to take those)—take a manifestation break rather than a coffee break.

These intuitive manifestation boards, whether physical or digital, are not finite. As you set the questions, you release your intuitive hounds. As you start to choose the images or write down words, you will know through your tells whether this is right or whether this image or this word belongs here—lean into your "What's my YES, what's my NO?" Be selective, but remember you can edit and amend at any time.

Where you keep your board or writing is important because you need to continue to keep the dream alive and how you treat it represents the strength of your belief in it.

To affirm to your intuition that the board is on track or to realize that it needs changing, you should keep it somewhere you will see daily. At one of my first jobs, which I intuitively knew I wasn't meant to do for long (but had no clue about what I actually wanted to do) I knew I needed to invest my energy in keeping my ego cool and free from frustration in this space I spent most of my daily life—frustration looses intuitive flow afterall. So I used the inside of a cupboard door at my place of work that I opened more than once a day and I would add images for my future career here! Whenever I felt deflated, I would return to the image of what intuitively I had set my sights on. As technology advanced, I created a collage of pictures as my screen saver. Even though these wishes didn't come true all at once and some goals evolved, they did all come in time.

Remember to take time to check in on what you are creating. Come back to your question and your intuitive ask and use your tells to show you whether the images or the words are still right, or relevant for you. Let your intuition respond through your "YES" or "NO" body responders and your radiators and drain signifiers.

## WHEN TO BE DECISIVE AND WHEN TO THINK ON IT

Please remember what is truly meant for you will never pass you by, so take the pressure off yourself right now. Discard all the ego's chitter-chatter—those explanations as to why you should not, could not and never will. Also remember that changing your mind halfway through working toward a goal is OK. As we grow, our needs and desires change, evolve and grow with us, so don't be afraid or concerned if your intuition guides you to let go of something you thought you "wanted" so passionately at one stage of your life. If your ego appears, shouting loudly or wakes you up at night in fear of this letting go, come back to the grounding exercise (see page 210) to find your balance.

# Setting Intentions
# and Seeing Signs

So let's connect higher and sense for a higher source. Intuition is our faithful guide and our compass but it also lights the way for us to interact with the universe and the spirit. Now the universe or spirit, as with intuition, doesn't speak our verbal language, but it does commune with us through life and through our body—remember humans didn't always speak—we evolved, so why would we assume that speech is the highest form or only tool of communication?

The good news is we can learn how to use this language and to see our intuitive intentions manifest in the everyday and so we can plant and grow what we would like to experience or feel (opportunities, feelings, people or places, for example). It's also a friend you can work with in creating signs or signals (call them signs and signals of encouragement) that, with the help of the universe, will encourage you along the way, reminding you to "keep going" or to "slow down." These signs will help maintain focus, navigate your path and keep your spirits up when you slip into self-doubt or feel that a mental clock is ticking down.

Intention is everything, EVERYTHING, and we need to become aware of those conversations in our mind that are shaping our reality and interfering with our manifestations. There is one false statement we need to change to start shifting the intuitive gear away from ego's conversation—the age-old "I'll believe it when I see it" needs to transform into "I'll see it when I believe it."

# INTENTION-SETTING RITUAL

WHAT DO I WANT

WHAT DO I NEED

You will need a candle, an unlined blank piece of white paper or card as well as a pen or pencil.

Crystals can support this work and enhance the vibration:

- Clear quartz for clarity and focus

- Labradorite for knowing your heart's truth

- Amethyst or ametrine to stimulate your third eye

You may already have a dream and goal in mind, but it is important to start with no expectation of where you "need" to end up. Remember intention is everything, so start with "I let go of my expectations" (as ever repeating three times) as your opening line as we move into this exercise in your sacred space.

## 1/

Light a candle in your sacred space and place your card or paper between you and the candle. Place your hands down flat on either side of the paper.

## 2/

Sit quietly and focus on lengthening your breath while looking deeply into the flame—let your breath take you deep within as you connect with your intuition. Perhaps you see or feel that intuitive wheel and dial spinning or your tells all along your body start to prickle and pulse. Visualize all your thoughts pouring into the flame, letting them come, letting them go, let the flame consume them, letting yourself be and giving yourself the time to do so.

## 3/

Now turn your attention and your intuition inward and down toward your heart. Ask your heart to shine that light onto the answer that you are seeking your intuition's response to.

## 4/

Ask yourself what you're seeking today, this week, this year. What's your intention? To feel safe? To feel strong? To pull in more love? To feel more protected, more grounded? To feel an abundance of life, of love? Or to shine bright? The options are endless, just like you.

## 5/

Say the following mantra out loud three times, while your focus remains on the flame, as your mind clears and allows your heart a clear pathway to intuit "What do I want, what do I need?" Allow your personal intention, whether a word or a statement, to reach your lips, let a feeling roll over your entire being or a visual drift into your mind's eye. Remember nothing is too weird or crazy. Let intuition deliver it to you—let it form, trust it, and repeat it aloud, in your mind and in your heart.

6/

Repeat your intention as it comes to you, out loud three times. Allow your voice to give your intention words and allow your voice to become a bell ringing your intention out into the universe, out into life.

7/

Now write your intention down across the center of the card or paper and, in the bottom left-hand corner, write what your ask was.

8/

Watch the intention, the words on your card, with your human eyes before gently allowing your eyes to close, drawing the words or image to your mind's eye. On an exhalation, move the image up and out through your crown, the energy center at the top of your head, giving life to the intention by releasing it to your higher self and to the universe.

9/

Let it go, release it to that higher power by opening your eyes. Your intention (just like an email!) is now sent!

10/

Seal your intention practice in by repeating three times, "I am and I can, I ask, I believe and now I see."

Whenever you doubt your intention or manifestation, come back to the intention card you've created. Any time you want to add more strength and power to it, come back to it and repeat this mantra, this intention, out loud three times.

You can place your intention card somewhere that will catch your human eye—your bedside table, on your desk or on the fridge. I like to place mine around the house, but I also like to set an alert or a calendar reminder on my phone with the intention written in it, to go off at random times throughout the day, so when it goes off and I read the words of my intention, it sends a warmth to my intuition, a vibration that says "I hear you" as it replies "we got you."

To extend the practice and channel the intention with your intuition for a specific scenario, simply repeat the ritual and when you come to ask, "What do I want, what do I need?," add a specific question, for example, "What do I need to bring me closer to love?" or "What do I want, what do I need to find my purpose/my dream house/to be happier/to feel more connected?" Set your question and trust your intuition to drive it within your meditation. Write it down, encase it in love and bring it into your life.

It's best to start by doing one intention with your intuition at a time and, as you feel more confident, you can gather a few at a time, but

be aware that you can burn out spiritually too, driven by the same anxiety of trying to over-control everything in your life.

Please take care of each intention card you bring to life, too. Ensure that you write them all on the same size of card or piece of paper and handle them with care, for we are going to gather and grow our own deck of intention cards to use later in our practice.

# INTENTION-SETTING RITUAL
## at a glance

**Light a candle** in your sacred space and place your card or paper between you and the candle. Place your hands down flat on either side of the paper.

**Sit quietly and focus** on lengthening your breath while looking deeply into the flame—let your breath take you deep within as you connect with your intuition.

**Visualize** all your thoughts pouring into the flame, letting the flame consume them and letting yourself be.

**Now turn your attention** and your intuition inward and down toward your heart. Ask yourself what you're seeking today, this week or this year. What is your intention?

**Say the following mantra** out loud three times, "What do I want, what do I need?" Allow your personal intention to reach your lips. Let the feeling roll over your entire being or the visual drift into your mind's eye.

**Repeat your intention** out loud three times as it comes to you before writing it down on the card in front of you.

**Watch the intention**, the words on your card, with your human eyes before gently allowing your eyes to close, drawing the words to your mind's eye. On an exhalation, move the image up and out through the crown of your head, releasing it to your higher self and to the universe.

**Let it go**, release it to that higher power by opening your eyes. Your intention is now sent. (Just like an email!)

**Seal your intention** practice by repeating three times, "I am and I can. I ask, I believe and now I see."

Listen to
yourself,
get clearer
answers.

# WHAT IS MY SIGN?

Have I done this right? How do I know my intention is working?

Has somebody or something just rocked your faith in yourself? This fear or worry will be familiar to all of us, but we can use our intuition to help guide us. The work is more long-term and less about instant gratification, but we can we set some flags ahead of us to help us trust that we are navigating the way ahead through life correctly with our intuition.

Signs can be quirky or they can be straight down the line and crystal clear—sometimes so much so that we dismiss them. Intuition will decide how to get your attention and then place markers in your day (even in your dreams). If it's something that requires particular focus, it may place these signs in obscure locations to really get your attention because the sign will be such an anomaly that you won't miss it.

Move back into your sacred space with your intention cue card in your hand and the candle before you. If your intuition feels particularly open that day, you may not need to.

Focus on the words you've written on the cards, take your attention into your heart, awakening it and using it as a torch for your intuition. Repeat out loud three times, "What's my sign, my intuitive tell for this intention?" Close your eyes, like a camera closing its shutter and your intuition will imprint the answer in your mind's eye or whisper the sign into your body. Listen and feel for it.

Open your eyes as soon as you sense the response to "develop" it as though onto a camera film. Affirm the sign by saying aloud or in your mind, "And so it is." Write the sign in the top right corner of the card, if you wish.

A sign can be anything, from the shape of a heart—a symbol of love—to a star to signify your light. It can be a bird, feathers, numbers or letters. Sometimes signs find you before you even sit to set them. Before I wrote my first book, I kept seeing the letters EJ everywhere. I didn't know why but I started to write the date and time I saw the letters. For a time, I thought (my ego hoped!) they were the initials of someone I like, but then I received an email from a publisher whose initials are EJ. Nearly a year later, I set the intention to write another book and, sure enough, I started to see the same initials every day and a week later Elen wrote to me about this book.

If a sign finds you, it is crucial you don't overthink it. Come back to your space and ask your heart to shine a light onto what your intention wants to show or teach you. Let it flow to you as we've just practiced and we can now start to decipher them by using your intuition and your intuitive deck of cards.

# Your Intuitive
# Deck of Cards

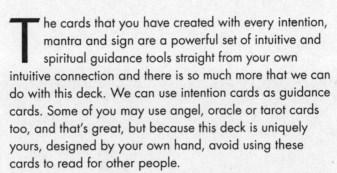

The cards that you have created with every intention, mantra and sign are a powerful set of intuitive and spiritual guidance tools straight from your own intuitive connection and there is so much more that we can do with this deck. We can use intention cards as guidance cards. Some of you may use angel, oracle or tarot cards too, and that's great, but because this deck is uniquely yours, designed by your own hand, avoid using these cards to read for other people.

Return to your sacred space and lay the cards with the words face down, in a line in front of you. Rub your hands together to stimulate the energy centers in your hands, which will become your super-sensors, take a breath and close your eyes. Float your dominant or writing hand above the cards and ask your intuition, "What's my YES, today?" Repeat this over and over as you move your hand along the line of cards. By now, you know what your "YES" tell is, so when you feel it, place your hand down on the card it is moving over. Turn the card over and reveal your answer or clarification.

You can, of course, start to add other words and statements to your deck, such as "yes," "no," "not yet," "have patience" but whenever you do this, always come to your intuition in your sacred space. Be wary of rushing this process and allowing your ego to write what you think you would like to hear.

4

·

# INTUITION
# FOR . . .

·

t's time to hone your intuitive hound into some more specifics, for the big drivers of our life such as your career, love, life purpose, for healing the past, connecting with who we really are. Do this in whatever order of importance you find in any time of your life . . . play with these exercises even if you don't need them right now; connecting to these practices with a clear headspace will prove invaluable when the tides of life unexpectedly turn.

So lets dive in, Intuition for . . .

W e're going to cover an important array of life topics in this next section, things we tend to turn to outside support to get the best advice for—but now is the time to lean toward ourselves and learn how we can use our intuition instead. Whether it's at work: how to get that job or push harder for that much-deserved pay increase; right through to honoring the most important relationship in your life—the one with yourself. We'll also work toward drawing in the energy of future love or deepening the love that's already in your life. This is intuition for the big stuff!

As well as going forward, we're also going to go back a little to heal intuitively all that which has passed and that is—knowingly or unknowingly—holding you back or holding you under. So prepare to get comfortable with the uncomfortable—remember, you have got this and I've got you!

# Big Life Decisions:
# Career, Work, Purpose

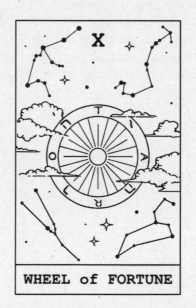

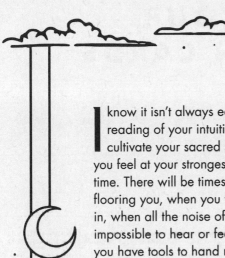

I know it isn't always easy to trust yourself, let alone your reading of your intuition. This is why it is important to cultivate your sacred space—a calm, cool space where you feel at your strongest, so that this trust can develop over time. There will be times when life feels like it's completely flooring you, when you feel completely unequipped to tune in, when all the noise of your mind is making it seemingly impossible to hear or feel for the right decision. Remember you have tools to hand no matter how crazy the storm.

The next two exercises are designed for use when you feel the decision is overwhelmingly big. And the first starts with what you have been building on already . . . your intuitive intention cards.

# PULLING YOUR INTENTION CARDS

I love to pull a range of spirit cards—sometimes I recognize that's my ego looking for my "perfect answer" and what I really need to do is tune in for the perfect intuitive feel and response. So what better way to do that than to delve in deeper and bring to life something you have already started to craft by hand: your very intuitive self.

**1/**

Come to your sacred space. Light a candle, come to the breath—a long breath in for a count of six, then a long breath out for a count of seven. Repeat five times.

**2/**

Shuffle your deck of cards with the question or matter at hand—say it aloud or write it down on a cue card and put it before you in order to apply more focus as you shuffle your deck.

**3/**

When you feel ready, lay the cards face down and spread them in a line or a circle, whichever feels right to you.

**4/**

Rub your hands together to stimulate a sensory connection with your intuition. Take your dominant or writing hand and start to move it along the line of cards or around the circle in a clockwise motion.

**5/**

Take your time. Move your hand slowly as you begin a conversation with your intuition, asking out loud,

"What do I want, what do I need, where shall I go in, show me what to follow?" Keep repeating this ask over and over and when your ask has been received, when it has been heard, you will feel a drop of heat or a heaviness at your belly. Bring your focus back to your hands.

**6/**

As you continue to move your hands slowly over the top of the cards, wait for a corresponding pulse or a prickle of energy between your hand and the card to show itself—that is an answer to your question from intuition. Place your hand down on that card.

**7/**

Turn it over and check how you feel by it—before you (or rather your ego) reject it—sit with it and really feel into that answer.

If you haven't yet built a deck of cards or you want to be more specific, you can come back to "YES," "NO" and "MAYBE" answers. However, in order to take this out of your ego's hands, write these three words on identical pieces of card so that you cannot see through the paper and create a bubble of doubt for yourself. Repeat the process just with these three answers.

Perhaps you have two choices in front of you, you're trying to choose between two jobs, for example. Take three pieces of card and in pencil write the name of each business on each of the cards and leave one blank. Repeat the card pull as above.

If you don't feel happy about the card pull, and this happens to all of us, investigate why. Sit with it and ask of your intuition whether it is your ego

that doesn't like this outcome? Don't reject the card. Instead, shuffle the cards, lay them out face-down and move the order around. Leave the room for a good five minutes before coming back to repeat the exercise with your intuitive presence.

Sometimes the answer can be found in your instant reaction to a "YES" or "NO" or to a name. Trust that. If you pull a business name and your gut turns with disappointment—that's intuition giving you a very clear answer.

# PULLING YOUR INTENTION CARDS
## at a glance

**Come to your sacred space.** Light a candle, come to the breath. Breathe in for a count of six, then out for a count of seven. Repeat five times.

**Shuffle** your deck of cards with the question or matter at hand. Say it aloud or write it down on a cue card and put it before you to apply more focus as you shuffle your deck.

**When you feel ready**, lay the cards face down and spread them in a line or a circle, whichever feels right to you.

**Rub your hands together** to stimulate a sensory connection with your intuition. Take your dominant or writing hand and start to move it along the line of cards or around the circle in a clockwise motion.

**Take your time.** Move your hand slowly as you ask out loud, "What do I want? What do I need? Where shall I go in? Show me what to follow." Keep repeating this ask over and over. When it has been received, you will feel a drop of heat at your belly. Bring your focus back to your hands.

**Continue to move your hands** slowly over the top of the cards, wait for a corresponding pulse or prickle of energy between your hand and the card to show itself—this is the answer from your intuition. Place your hand down on that card.

**Turn it over and check how you feel** by it before you (or your ego) reject it. Sit with it and feel your way into that answer.

# INTUITIVE VIEWING

This next exercise has been created and energetically charged (yes that's right we can charge symbols) to help you raise your intuition up clearly into your mind's eye (or third eye or however you know it)—let go and go see!

1/

Come to your sacred space and light a candle. Come to your breath and place your right hand within the illustration on the next page as indicated. Put your left hand on your heart and focus on the center of the spiral mandala, repeating this meditation: "I ask my intuition to let me see, let flow to me what will be." Repeat five times.

2/

Feel a blanket of energy move over your body and warmth fill you from within. This is your intuition connecting with your highest self and the energies of the universe. This might make you feel sleepy, but refrain from lying down on your back as you carry out this exercise.

3/

Start to follow the spiral line around the illustration, until your human eyes become heavy. If they close, let them connect deep into your mind's eye. If your eyes remain open, keep them fixed in focus on the center point of the maze. Allow yourself to travel with your intuition. If you feel stuck, start to follow the lines once again, and then over and over until you feel you are focused on this and nothing more—let it take you beyond your mind's imagination.

What you see will be unique to you. I cannot give you an idea of what to expect because it will be the work of your intuition, not mine. You will know that you have completed your intuitive viewing when the room starts to feel real. The protective heaviness that came from your intuition as you connected with the universe's energy, with spirit energy, will clear and leave you wide awake and ready for action.

Please write it down or audio record yourself. Don't overthink or over-analyze—let it be for now. Let intuition show you, be that today, tomorrow or further ahead.

You have got
this and your
intuition
has got
you.

# Having a Better Relationship with Yourself

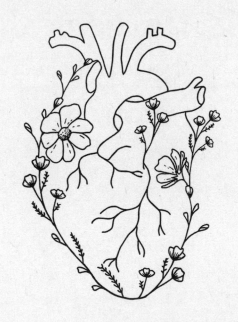

We're so often told not to make things "all about you" because it's arrogant and self-centered, so we shy away from it and when we do need to think about ourselves, we apologize for it. But, as with all things, it's the context that's important. More and more people are seeking help and guidance from spiritual, faith or energy healers, readers and guides or taking self-development courses, hoping for assurance that they're on the right track—for affirmation that they are a good person who is capable of making the right decisions for themselves. But they are reaching out rather than reaching in and you need a balance or at least a little of both. I believe, though, that the only way out, the only real way through a tough time is to look inside ourselves first, so this section is dedicated to you and the power of your inner child, and unleashing your magic back into yourself.

# RECONNECTING WITH YOUR INNER CHILD

Your inner child is that part of your intuition that's known you since birth. It's the purest form of you and it nurtures you, helping you grow and find your path—in your career, personal growth or in your relationships. It's the part of you that feels fearless and strong, ready to take a stand when you need to and it can even warn us of stormy waters ahead, so we can navigate a safe path to a harbor.

When we have been knocked or abandoned (in any sense), our inner child can go into hiding and we lose faith in our ability to direct our future. Reconnecting with your inner child is about reconnecting with your most intuitive self and rediscovering your true self so you can live a fulfilling life.It's about getting back to what feels natural and what feels good. There are no rules, just your spirit, your intuition and yourself!

I recommend working with crystals because their energies and vibrations act as a filter that allows you to sink deeper into an intuitive state while also releasing out stagnant energy and simultaneously drawing in universal energy into your energy centers and your body. This helps you to declutter and connect deeper with the part of your intuition that roams free and dreams without boundaries. Crystals also allow you to heighten your feelings and soothe your emotions—a perfect match for your sensitive inner child who picks up on everything! Try amazonite, rose quartz, celestite and tiger's eye for this next exercise. Amazonite allows you to play and grow without limitation, rose quartz offers a protective energetical glow, celestite has a connection to all things outside and tiger's eye is for confidence.

You will need some paper or a notebook, four crystals (such as those mentioned above or four of your own choosing) and a photo of you as a kid that invokes from within you a smile of pure joy. This can be from any age or time, but it should be a picture of you without other people, so that you don't pull in anybody else's energy.

Come to your sacred space and light a candle for more focused intention, if you wish. Your body will feel heavy with this exercise and you will need room to readjust, so have a cushion to support your spine. In time, you'll be able to do this on the move, even sitting on a bus, but for now relax and get comfortable.

Lay three of the crystals (use your intuition to pick which feels right to you) onto the picture in a triangle formation around the image of you, preferably focused around your face. I say three crystals because three is a powerful number and you will notice I use it a lot in each exercise to empower the intentions, or mantras— the number three represents the manifestation of creation, inspiration and growth, while also symbolizing the beautiful connection between your mind, body and spirit. It is also powerfully aligned to the universe and divine energy. Lay them intuitively. There is no right or wrong here, the order they go in is not important. Just let them connect and vibrate as nature allows. Take the fourth stone (of your intuitive choosing) into your non-dominant hand.

Now for the call and response. We are going to call our inner intuitive child, just as we do when we call to our tells, although this time we are working with six calls for attention. I have made some suggestions and guides for your calls, but as always feel free to create or expand your own. Over time you'll just tap into trusting what you want to ask as much as you trust your intuition's response.

Place the fourth crystal in your non-dominant hand, come to focus on your photo, the image of you. Come to the breath, connect to intuition via your circle, your dial or however feels best. Allow yourself to sense and feel the crystal energy pulsing or vibrating, calling to you, and allow this energy to connect with you and your intuition as you recite three times out loud or in your mind: "It's time for me to come to play, to tap in deep to hear what my inner intuitive child has to say."

Allow the crystal's energy to vibrate, transporting you to the magic within your intuitive inner child. A smile or tear may cross your face; this is OK, it's just the connection deepening. Allow yourself to feel the crystal, pulsing and connecting, taking you deeper into the self. Say the calls aloud, with closed eyes if you can. You can also read them and then close your eyes—it will all come with practice.

The following calls are for different times of inquiry in your life, when you are asking or seeking to understand—remember to repeat each three times.

## WHO YOU ARE

### INTUITIVE CALL

"Is what I am and what I see helping me to remember how to truly be me?"

## TO KNOW YOUR DESIRES AND NEEDS

### INTUITIVE CALL
"Dear sweet innocence of self—what treats in life do you need to make us connect at greater speed?"

## ASKING ABOUT RELATIONSHIPS OR FRIENDS

### INTUITIVE CALL
"Loyalty, my friend, is a must, to whom should I embrace and hold in my trust?"

## FOR A GREATER SENSE OF SELF

### INTUITIVE CALL
"Just as a fire burns so bright please show me what I need to heighten my own light."

## FOR INNER DRIVE

### INTUITIVE CALL
"Creative stimulation is the key, allow me to surrender and to understand what truly drives me."

## FOR HEALING AND FOR GROWTH

### INTUITIVE CALL:
"Here in life, I feel ready to go, but some bumps and bruises have heeded my flow. Now It's time to heal, time to grow, so please reveal what I need to let go."

Remember, take this slow and steady, one question at a time. Let your intuitive response rise, whether in visuals, storytelling in your mind's eye, a feeling, a sensation or a knowing—let it all come powerfully to you. When intuition has finished answering your call, once more you will feel the room around you.

Give yourself a break (which can be minutes or days) between each question and between recording and reviewing your responses from your

THE LIFE-CHANGING POWER OF INTUITION

inner child. Remember this is not an interrogation, but a connection with your seemingly hidden self.

You can write each one out on your paper or in your notebook—at the top of a page, with space to record your responses if that also feels good to you.

How we receive and channel our intuition works in the most wonderfully unique ways—some of us will free-write (and sometimes all over the page), some will feel the urge to doodle, paint or draw their responses out quite literally. Sometimes I hear it in song or whisper while I am writing or sketching. Our intuition uses all our senses to speak to us, so don't ignore or reject any of its signs and know

that however you start is not where it will finish. Let the creative collage unfold from within you to enlighten you.

Remember throughout to focus on the self and build your intuition muscle—check in with your tells as they will also be guiding you throughout each practice. If we rush past these basics, we head straight into our ego and what it wants to know, and that loud, shouty voice drowns out our inner child and our intuition once again. In time, with practice and patience, you will be able to differentiate these voices and use this practice to answer any question, no matter how big or how small.

The road to
self-discovery
starts HERE.

# For Seeing and Healing
# Who You Really Are

In order to connect more deeply to your intuition, you have to connect to a deeper sense of self—who you are at your purest essence. That is why you need to find your inner child, who is who you were before life told you who to be. You need to create a space to "see" who you really are and to cleanse away any harsh comparisons with others that you carry, judgments of self, old warn-out habits from the mind that have made you feel as though you are not good enough.

# MIRROR, MIRROR RITUAL

Nothing is more uncomfortable than the fear you drive deep into your self and your body, your mind. By comparing yourself to others or even a previous version of yourself, you are dampening your spirit and taking away the power from your own voice—your intuition.

What you will be creating here is a crystal mirror, which will offer you a heightened reflection, one with a tender healing vibration, one that comes bathed in respect and love for you and that shows what you really need to see, cleansing you of fear or worn thought patterns.

You will need some of your favorite crystals, a glass bowl, rose oil, palo santo wood or incense (not sage this time—it's too harsh for this gentle and nurturing exercise), a mirror (one that ideally is mounted on a wall) and some water.

Use your intuition to find the mirror that is best for this exercise, just as you did when locating your sacred space. Ask, listen and look. Is it the one in your bathroom or bedroom or hallway? If your intuition is leading you toward another room or another space, you can move your mirror, but make sure you can keep your hands free.

Fill your glass bowl with cold water. I have picked a mix of crystals, here, but feel free also to mix and match your own.

**Crystals:** rose quartz, peridot, labradorite, moon stone, aragonite, apache tears/black obsidian. Polished or raw, little or large—whatever your intuitive preference.

Place the crystals into the bowl of water and place the bowl underneath or next to your mirror. Light the palo santo wood and waft it through the air carefully, moving the stick between yourself and the mirror as if you were rubbing away pencil marks from paper. This is to clear the energy and rid the space of any negative associations and thoughts that might come to you when you look in the mirror.

You can call as always to intuition here to assist you, out loud or in your mind: "The space is now clear, the space is now kind, the view is now clear, the view is now kind." And so it is . . .

With one hand touching the surface of the water, call to your intuition again as you look deep into the mirror:

*"Dear intuition, please hear my gentle call for you to . . . please cleanse my thoughts and heal my mind, allow me to see and feel all that is mine to shine.*

*What has come, what others may show, I will celebrate but not use to interrupt my own joyous flow."*

Repeat three times.

Take a moment to let old thoughts and fears flash before your eyes, through your mind, your mind's eye as they shift out and through your body and being—let go of all those things that you want to let go of. Your intuition will indicate what to ditch and what to nourish through visuals, through feelings—through your tells. Let the thoughts come, let them go. Hold your gaze in the mirror and your touch on the water—let it hold you safe, hold you steady. Allow your intuition to rise up from your belly, up through the heart into the third eye chakra and out through the crown center—as always use your breath to assist it.

If your mind is prone to drifting, set a timer for three minutes. Hold your reflection, even when it feels uncomfortable. Breathe. Allow yourself to see the complete you, bathed in love, held in the loving

crystal vibration. When doubt slides in, and it often will, repeat to yourself:

*"This is real, this is happening."*

and

*"I surrender to see my love."*

The visuals, words or situations associated with what you are releasing will be cleansed by the crystal mix and their loving vibration—think of them as your hoover for any negative thought, emotion or action. They will allow you to acknowledge and affirm how things really are or how you wish them to be.

Come to close your practice when the timer ends or when you feel ready—your hand in the water will send a signal to your free hand, like a shock or a flash of heat, a feeling of clarity or weight— remember this will be unique to you. If you are asking yourself if it is over, yes, it is.

Take a breath here before you

leave and note down or record what arose. Release five drops of the rose oil into the water to seal in your healed reflection and to set how you are to be seen by yourself and others in life from here on in (and not just in your sacred space). Make it your intention to see yourself like that every time you see your reflection. If you do write down your feelings, fold them and place them under the bowl or pop your notebook underneath it.

Leave the crystal mirror in place for three days and nights. On the fourth day, remove the crystals one by one and dry them on the windowsill in natural light (daylight or moonlight). If you can, pour the water outside onto the earth or on a plant to signify a deepened connection with life, nature and growth—remember our earthing elemental power.

When the crystals are dry, you can leave them by the mirror or take out on the road with you to empower and fuel you as you go. They'll not only serve as reminders of your intentions but allow you to hold on to that powerful healing frequency, so that intuition can remind you who you are, where and why you are, wherever you are.

# TAKING IT TO THE NEXT LEVEL

After you have practiced this exercise a few times, try using the water in the bowl instead of the mirror to reflect yourself and to see deeper with your intuitive eye. Start the exercise as you did before, but this time look and focus at your face in the water instead of the mirror. This time place your dominant hand around the side of the bowl instead of inside it.

Here are some other healing mixes and calls for you to take to the mirror. These calls to intuition are more focused, tailored to different moods or situations that you may find yourself in, when you are fighting to come back to self and in need of intuitive flow.

## FOR WHEN YOUR HEAD'S IN A SPIN:

**Crystals:** amethyst, howlite, apatite, black tourmaline in the water and opal by the side of and touching the glass bowl

**Supporting essential oil:** lavender, bergamot or rose otto

**Meditation:**
"Ground me, guide me, give me strength to find the truth inside me."

## WHEN YOU NEED TO DETOX FROM ANGER:

**Crystals:** aventurine, amethyst, amazonite, amber, rainforest jasper

**Supporting essential oil:** myrrh or jasmine

**Meditation:**
"Let it be, let it go—free me from this anger shadow,
Move me back wholehearted to my intuitive flow."

## TO RELEASE WORRY AND FEAR:

**Crystals:** turquoise, tiger's eye, jet, moonstone, iolite, labradorite

**Supporting essential oil:** lavender

**Meditation:**
"When I look to the future, let the now be all I see
As I ask for the worry and fear to step aside from me.
So I can see it as it is and why I am triggered,
Let my gut guide me to understand, to get this figured."

FOR WHEN YOU'RE LOOKING FOR JOY:

**Crystals:** aventurine, citrine (three pieces if possible), crazy lace agate, clear quartz

**Supporting essential oil:** bergamot or geranium

**Meditation:**
"Let me mix it, craft it, drink it all up,
Forever be flowing from a joy-filled cup.
Life is a blessing—a fun lesson to be learned
So I light it up knowing my own self, I won't burn."

FOR WHEN YOU WISH TO FEEL THE ENERGY OF LOVE CLEARER AND LOUDER:

**Crystals:** rose quartz, rhodochrosite, peridot, prasiolite, sunstone

**Supporting essential oil:** neroli

**Meditation:**
"Love is louder when I make it,
So here today is the path I am taking.
Let it drive me to commit me to what I deserve,
And allow always, my heart to be heard."

These healing mixes are to recalibrate your entire being with intuition when life knocks you. They are not for overthinking or self-criticism, but self-compassion. As always, note down how you feel after you have finished your practice. Is intuition sending you signs or tells? Or you can just go and chill—whatever feels right to you!

You need to create a space to "see" who you really are.

# For Improving Relationships with Your Friends and Family

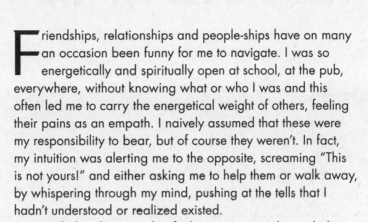

Friendships, relationships and people-ships have on many an occasion been funny for me to navigate. I was so energetically and spiritually open at school, at the pub, everywhere, without knowing what or who I was and this often led me to carry the energetical weight of others, feeling their pains as an empath. I naively assumed that these were my responsibility to bear, but of course they weren't. In fact, my intuition was alerting me to the opposite, screaming "This is not yours!" and either asking me to help them or walk away, by whispering through my mind, pushing at the tells that I hadn't understood or realized existed.

I ended up losing sight of where everyone else ended (energetically and emotionally) and where I began because I hadn't learned how to honor my intuition or myself. Without awareness, understanding or training, we have no idea how to hold this space; whether to heal it intuitively or instead to send energy to another intuitively to help them heal it for themselves.

So, I recommend that you attract an energy that matches your own rather than working with intuition to align yours with someone else's. We all want to heal, but to feel love is to help someone awaken their own energy, showing them how by example and not carrying it for them or forcing them there.

I use the next exercise, the circle of light, weekly (daily when I need to), to give myself and my intuition a space to hold hands and grow in alignment; to allow intuition to show me who I should be surrounding myself with and who I need to move back from; to look at my roles, in family, friendship groups, relationships, work and beyond.

# THE CIRCLE OF LIGHT

Until you become well practiced in this exercise, keep your eyes open and allow the words on the page to guide you, or record yourself reading the instructions step by step and play it back as a guide.

1/
Come to sit comfortably in your sacred space, with palms face up and open to receiving, as we come to focus on the breath.

2/
Breathe in and out through the nose: in for a count of five, out for a count of seven, and repeat. Let the count become your focus. A candle flame can be helpful or you can use a dalmatian stone or rose quartz crystal (crystals whose vibe is set to promote and stimulate loyalty and trust) as a focus point for your human eyes, letting them focus and fixate, while your third eye or mind's eye opens.

3/
Start to bring your awareness in toward your heart on an inhalation for the count of five; as you exhale (for a count of seven), move your awareness down to focus on the belly and your solar plexus. Repeat seven times.

4/
As you repeat this breathing cycle, your eyes soften, your breath now moves into the heart and out to the belly effortlessly without thought, without the need to count. Let this motion rock you like a gentle wave in the sea. Choose now, with your heart and intuition those who you'd like to inquire about today: lovers, family, friends, those to come or those who have gone . . .

5/
Start to sense, visualize or feel a white light forming at your mind's eye or third eye on each inhalation and exhalation. It may have a texture much like that of a cloud—fluffy, light comforting. With every round of breath as this light grows, your body now simultaneously begins to root into the earth beneath you and you will sense and feel this at your base chakra, where your buttocks touch the ground.

6/
This light begins to expand more widely now as you inhale, creating a circle of light that encompasses your entire body before it very gently starts to move back away from your body and out into the room but also into the space you gently find yourself within in your mind's eye.

7/

When the light has expanded to its fullest potential, it now starts to move with every breath. The cloud of light moves further back and away from you and, as it does, it starts to clear the view before you within your mind's eye—you are starting to see with clear intuitive insight. Feel yourself sitting within your mind's eye in a place of comfort that flows from your intuition to you. Notice the quality of the ground you are sitting on. Notice what needs tending to, what's overgrown, what's ready for planting. This is your resting place, your healthy comfort zone, a place to nurture your relationships weekly with intuitive insight and wisdom. The cloud light has formed a protective and strong energy ring around you and you feel safe sitting within its bubble.

8/

As you continue to focus on the breath, you may start to hear or feel them first—a line of friends, family, past and present, coming in closer to the edge of the protective cloud of light. If you feel anxious or overly excited, come back to the breath. Remember that you are not alone here, intuition has safeguarded your space with the cloud of light and no one can climb over it or run through it—they can only be invited in by mutual agreement between intuition and you.

9/

At your invitation, the people you are inquiring about (sometimes three may come at once, so allow intuition to lead you to the person you should start your work with) step through the protective cloud of light.

10/

Allow yourself to feel how your intuition has embodied itself within your mind's eye at this time—remember your tells, your signs, and allow intuition to manifest however is right to you today.

11/

Watch how it shows itself to you—as a bird or animal, as a body of light or energy, a symbol or a feeling of a person you know or as a part of yourself. Ask of intuition now, out loud or in your mind, "Dear intuition—whom do we need to first shine upon with your light?" Repeat three times.

**12/**

You sense and feel yourself remaining seated and grounded, not only in your safe space but within the cloud of light within your mind's eye, watching as intuition now steps behind one of the beings in your space. Allow them to be known to you and allow intuition to show you what needs healing or releasing in this relationship or what is required for its growth. Allow it to play out before you—just keep watching.

**13/**

You can ask your Intuition freely about the person before you:

- "Is this person right for me?"
- "What does this person, this relationship bring to me?"
- "Why do I feel uncomfortable when in this person's energy/company?"
- "What needs to heal here?"
- "How do I truly feel or see this person?"
- "What am I hiding from this connection?"

**14/**

You'll know intuitively what you want to ask before you ask it—there's no need to prepare, just trust that intuition will show you for your highest good and that you are ready to see that whatever the outcome.

**15/**

Allow your breath to release the need to fight the answer. Remember our chant from the energy cleanse and the chakra meditation and use it whenever you need: repeat "I am and I can" as you move back to remembering why or what has led you to this space, this line of inquiry. Allow yourself to be as brave as you are, brave enough to witness it, brave enough to trust in your intuitive viewing.

**16/**

Take time to offer this person what you both need—forgiveness, healing, love, peace, respect, release. You can say out loud or in your mind "I forgive you, I forgive myself, I send you and me healing love as we both now take the peace we deserve. I respect myself enough to release the need to experience this pain, this situation. I release the fear to the light and I bravely and gently move on." Embrace them energetically with your intuition and then move on to the next person of interest, watching as your intuition moves to stand behind them and repeat steps 12–15 until intuition has shone light upon every being in your protective circle.

## 17/

Now, if someone has hurt you unforgivably and your heart starts to feel as if it's clamping down and anxiety is racing in as you see them—this is super-important—you can choose to heal with intuition without rewatching the details of the relationship or the argument (you can always come back here at a later date if you decide to). Ask intuition to cover this person from the feet up to the top of their head in a blanket or cocoon of light, so no more harm can come to you from this person, situation, memory or energy and no more anger or hate will be offered back to them or reverberate off you. That energy is precious and they deserve your forgiveness because you deserve the peace.

## 18/

If someone is shown to you who is not familiar to you, this is a future relationship or a connection that requires a level of healing on your side in order to manifest or draw in this person deeper to your life. Do not run away from the unknown. Perhaps your heart's been bruised before and needs to heal to draw in a new flame or you've lost your confidence at work and doubt your ability to climb higher. Ask your intuition to show you who this is or what is needed to allow this person's light to step positively into your life.

## 19/

When the time has come, when all is soothed or healed as needs to today, right here right now, intuition will step in front of those gathered before you today. Intuition will then lovingly lead them back behind the outer edge of the circle of light, back into the cloud. Feel that circle once more. If someone is lingering in your inner circle, all you need do is to ask three times "Please step back now and out of my space" and they must and they will.

**20/**
Take time to see the clarity of your energy field—how it shines, how strong and how your work here today has enforced its strength and in turn your own.

**21/**
Intuition moves back toward you now, standing behind you, stepping into you, embodying you once again. Now affirm in your heart and mind "This is real, this is happening—all is healed, all is allowing for our highest good, all is well." Repeat this three times. Feel that clarity of connection, which is your own personal energy bodyguard.

Remember that intuition will and can change from day to day, practice to practice, situation and people. Sometimes my intuition appears as my grandfather Eric, who has passed, or shows as a butterfly, sometimes even a blue and yellow light, sometimes a visual or a word! We are ever-changing and intuition will change with you, it will join you "where you are at," so take good note of how they arrived on this day; these are signs that you can use to

deepen your setting intentions and seeing signs practice from page 118.

A friendly warning! Don't let your mind and ego force you into trying to see more. This can be exhilarating stuff but it's also tiring and you are working harder, deeper than you perhaps yet realize. You need time to digest it rather than over-analyze. Remember intuition is love, goodness, kindness. Fear, anger, worry and hate are all part of the ego and that is not who you are.

Know also that this intuitive energy space that you have now created is held for you in your every waking day, it is a protective space just for and of you, made of your energy and that of the universe that surrounds you. Not just in your mind's eye, it is a space that intuition will use to feel for you, to sense people out. It will allow only those whom you need in your everyday life at that time and will move away from your life, gently and at the right pace, those who no longer do.

If someone walks into your space who intuition does not deem right, when you are in the office, on the bus or on your social media, you will feel tiny warning electric shots as tells, like jellyfish stings rippling lovingly through the body. Before you let them step in too far, take a breath and ask in your mind (three times over) "Please step back and out of my space now into the light." Come back to your circle of light when the day is done (you could even do this in the bathroom at work or wherever you find yourself) and delve deeper into why this person flipped your switch in this way (even if they are a stranger). Ask yourself this in your own safe time, when you can respond properly to it with intuition rather than react to it with ego.

Finally, when bringing life to your circle of light, you may wish to use music to create a loving, peaceful support.

Ask yourself:
what's really
mine and what's
everyone else's.

# For Romance
# and Love

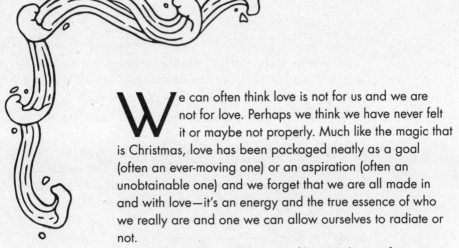

We can often think love is not for us and we are not for love. Perhaps we think we have never felt it or maybe not properly. Much like the magic that is Christmas, love has been packaged neatly as a goal (often an ever-moving one) or an aspiration (often an unobtainable one) and we forget that we are all made in and with love—it's an energy and the true essence of who we really are and one we can allow ourselves to radiate or not.

Intuition rides on the wave of love and on its frequency and vibration. It can help us move toward those whose intention is to care for us and bathe us in love. It also moves us out of harm's way, from those who will not be loving to us.

Love is an incredible learning tool, but it doesn't always have to be hard work or confusing. We can use intuition to hone in on the type of love we deserve to feel (rather than what we think we want) but take note—we cannot use it to shape, dominate or control another's value or shape of love. To do this would be a vain attempt at using love as a weapon of our ego and a dangerous one at that. In these cases, we have to compromise in love and, if that feels forced rather than flowing, we have to be brave and ask intuition to show us when to move away from a relationship that is no longer serving either of us.

We know that we attract into our lives what we vibrate or give out intuitively into life or to the universe, and we will meet a partner who reflects that back to us. So often we choose what we want in a relationship by how we think it should look—from magazines, Disney fairytales and the stories of love people have sugar-coated before us. Instead we have to decide how love feels best to us, so we can ensure we are honoring that for ourselves rather than abandoning it when someone comes along that we try to "fit" into our lives or we into theirs. Never forget that love is who we all are—love is kind, generous, gentle and good, and we have to learn how to flow with love, rather than force it.

●

# We can use intuition to hone in on the type of love we deserve to feel.

●

# A LETTER ON LOVE FROM YOUR HEART

We need to write a letter from the heart with intuition at hand to allow us to see bravely what we really want from love (rather than what we think we want) and then allow ourselves to honor that with intuition.

**1/**

Come to your sacred space with a few clean sheets of paper. Rose quartz and clear quartz (for clarity and unconditional love) are your crystal supports in this process, if you so wish, and will allow intuition to rise from the heart over ego and its sidekick fear.

**2/**

Place your left hand over your heart and right hand on top of that. Come to the breath (however feels right to you today, count your breaths or just lengthen them). Gently close your eyes and say aloud "Dear heart, my intuitive mind, please allow my past disappointments of love to come out and into the light." Repeat three times.

**3/**

Allow past disappointments to begin to rise or flutter into your mind's eye or third eye and blow them up and out through your crown, like a whale squirting out water from its blowhole—you may need to do this for at least three breaths just to clear the way comfortably and to connect deeper with intuition in this space. It's not unusual to laugh or cry or both at this time—either way these are great reactions, your body is releasing the vibe of that memory that's kept your heart prisoner for all that time.

**4/**

Begin to visualize or sense a green ball of light at your heart, sealed in with a fine pink light. Feel the beat of your heart respond to your call against your hands as your mind completely clears.

**5/**

Surrender to your intuition once more with a long, soothing inhalation through the nose and exhalation out of the mouth as you pull your hands away from your heart and gently toward the paper. Lay them down flat upon the paper and say aloud "Dear heart, my intuitive mind—please allow me to shine light on what in love I deserve to find." Repeat three times.

**6/**

Open your eyes and take pen to paper as you then write:

*Dear heart, my intuitive mind,*

*I know I have often wandered, left you feeling blind when it comes to bringing love to my side. But here today I channel, I flow and allow your words, your truths, your values, to this here page flow.*

*With love, in love,*

*Me*

Take a breath and write as you state out loud one of the following statements, depending on your current status:

WHEN SEEKING NEW LOVE

*"The call is heard, it is answered— may love bring you . . ."*

Or

WHEN IN A RELATIONSHIP

*"The call is heard, here now it is answered—let us show you where love can enrich you deeper."*

After each statement, let your heart and intuition flow through your hand and out through the pen. Allow what it wills for you to flow onto the paper. It might be specific. It may say or show you in your mind's eye love, without baggage. It may say height is important or that kindness is. Hear it and watch where your mind allows you to hesitate—that's your ego telling you you're not worthy and you could "never have that." Come back to intuition by repeating "I am, I can" and "This is real, this is happening." Let it all flow.

7/
Write until you are exhausted and no more words flow. Now sign the letter off as follows:

*I affirm that I here today allow intuition and the great powers, energies that be, to swim out and into the world to find what is truly resonating with me.*

*And so it is, and so I will honor it to be.*

*With love,*

*Me*

8/

Take the time to have a cup of tea and read your letter back to yourself, your heart and your intuition. Don't read it every day—let it come back to you. We can overdo our intention and put too much pressure on the how and when, slipping into ego with all its impatience and pressure on time. Remember we have to allow intuition to lead us there but also allow intuition, the universe and spirit to ready what (or rather who) is coming to you to rise up to meet you on a mutual level. Keep the letter, as with all manifestations. Perhaps you need to place it where you can see it or add it to your sacred space, maybe it's in a book of romantic poems or love letters, wherever feels best for you, so that you can nod to your manifestions in the making but not over-force them. I keep all my letters of the heart in a glass bottle (yes a message in a bottle) by my bed, so I can see it, nod to it, but not force or become frustrated by it. It's in my eyeline and I give life to it, and I give intuition's force to it by looking at it and placing my hands, left under right, at my heart when I do.

If you are already in a relationship, use your intuitive tells to advise you on how to tread forward. If you find yourself feeling deflated in your relationship, as if love has been lost, please come back to intuition and the circle of light for a deeper inquiry about how to rekindle this love or what to do next, but first do some self-reflective intuitive work (see the mirror, mirror ritual on page 154) or some energy cleansing, such as our chakra cleanse and connection meditation (see page 96)—a little intuitive self-healing goes a long way. Remember intuition is about the feel of love so let it fill you up with love as your relationship develops and grows, and know that you deserve it.

You deserve the
love you were
born to
make.

# For Healing
# the Past

Tuning in to your intuition is incredibly healing, but it can shine light on some monsters that have lingered in the depths within you. Life and your spirit try to show us these wounds or vulnerabilities through life lessons or they are reflected back to us in other people. What we tend to learn is to find a way to cope with it, deal with it to a certain extent or sweep it under the carpet in its entirety. Things that happened to me at school have echoed in different guises throughout my life experience—I had a terrible fear of being seen and judged; at that time I found the best way to express my emotions was through song. My mum sent me to singing lessons aged eleven and I loved it—and still do now—it is a great expressive tool for me, it also really helps me when I am channeling spirit. But while it gave me a release, a way to express myself and release tension, I never really dealt with my real fear of myself and my own voice. The singing was helpful, but I was using someone else's words to express my own emotion before I eventually realized that I needed to find, name and honor my own.

Intuition taught me how to listen to myself and it also taught me how to hold steady when the winds of my emotions or fear started to batter me and I'd like to gift that to you now.

# CORRECTING THE MEMORY FILM

We all know this story. The one where we feel bright with life and then in swoops the rain, be that a trigger to a memory of the past alerting itself in your today or someone saying something a certain way that takes us back to "that time when . . ." and it dampens our day and that's what we remember. But this time, let's pause the film before it plays out and re-edit it as it should be—to replay the good and shine light on it. This is an exercise for when the tears are stuck behind your eyes and/or when shock leaves you powerless. When the way ahead only looks dark and downward . . . we can lighten and shine.

Come to your sacred space which today will become your intuitive editing room. You will need:

- Your mind as the camera
- A large white candle and its flame as the lights
- Your mind's eye or third eye as your projector
- Your lines "This is real, this is happening." You can write this on a piece of paper and place between you and the candle

## YOUR CRYSTAL SUPPORT CAST

Crystals will always aid us by holding a higher vibration for us within our safe space. You don't have to use them, but should you wish to, I suggest:

**Citrine:** the abundance-maker, drawing in whatever it is you seek to attract

**Labradorite:** the heart reflector, shining your inner truths to the outside world

**Selenite:** for a heavenly lift

**Amethyst:** to open your mind and stimulate it, connecting to your highest good and calming the ego

**Aventurine:** for a feeling of adventure

You can of course also choose your own!

You will need about two pieces of each of these crystals, depending on the size of your candle because the crystals need to encircle the candle while touching each other.

Stage notes: You are moving toward giving intuition full ownership and you need to demote the old ego, but it will put up a bit of a fight— remember your ego thinks it's fighting for you!

## ACTION

### 1/
Come to your sacred space and place your crystals in a circle around the candle, making sure that they

are touching each other. Light the candle.

## 2/

Come to sit in front of the flame, watching its texture and depth as well as its flicker, color and the shapes that start to dance before your eyes. Allow yourself to become bewitched by it.

## 3/

Your breath starts to deepen, but not so that you are floating away, unlike some of the other exercises. Your eyes should be open as presence is required here, at first.

## 4/

Your mind will start to churn the story of the pain or the annoyance or memory at hand. Sit with it as it is here that we will start to project this story or this memory into the flame. Watch the flame now and project with your intention, your memory out into the light, so that it melts in its power. If you cannot "see" it, come to your other sense—feel it, intuitively sense it—use your tells to confirm when you ask them. Patience is key here because you are projecting the

pain away and surrendering it to the flame whereas the ego wants to keep it locked up inside you. Let them battle it out.

## 5/

Once the memory or situation has played out over and over until your mind is exhausted and frustrated, honor it—sit, breathe, start to accept that it has happened—that only intuition, the universe, spirit and you can change what you do with this memory next.

## 6/

Time to call deeper to intuition now. Come to visualize or feel the intuitive circle or dial as you connect to intuition. Control moves over effortlessly to intuition and you will feel it swell through your entire body and being as intuition fills you completely. This pinch or pressure point is also your "splice" point. Come now to this as the heat rises within you, reciting your lines in your mind or aloud, "This is real, this is happening." Repeat three times as always (remember disbelief is one of our ego's greatest allies).

**7/**
With your eyes still open, start to visualize wild horses riding in the candle flame. Take note of the color, observe their every detail. Allow your eyes to close if you so wish here and visualize the horses in the flame within your mind's eye—you are still watching the horses ride forward through your mind. Let them ride until they are clear of your mental screen of your mind and out of the picture, as you see your intuitive self standing ahead of you in the light of the flame with arms wide open, smiling. Notice the colors that the intuitive you is wearing, what is at their feet, what's in their hands—see all the detail and take note.

**8/**
Follow the actions of the intuitive you in your mind's eye. Allow them to show you what needs to be spliced as they move into your memory and flag to you through any feelings and sensations in your body, through your tells or in imagery in your mind's eye just what needs to be healed and how, in order to allow you to move forward. What intuition is drawing or projecting over your current scene,

your old memory, your mind will tell you is not possible, that it is making it up and that things cannot change. But you can reset the balance and recut your movie to have a happy ending.

**9/**
When your intuition is finished, when the changes of healing or moving forward have overlaid the pain of past or present, you will feel that the tension that was there before when you watched this scene over and over is now held there in love and the flow of intuition into your mind's eye will gently stop. Your eyes will tickle and your awareness of your body and your sacred place will be strong—it will feel as though a heat has been removed from your body and a sobering feeling of reality has re-entered the room, like when the lights come on at the end of the film in the cinema.

**10/**
Your ego will try to re-analyze the details and become the critic or film its own ending. You will feel the difference in directorship. Notice now when the memory or situation plays out in your

mind how you feel emotionally—how you can watch it without fear. Open your eyes if they are closed. Perhaps a little feeling of the sadness will linger, so cleanse yourself (see page 106) or open the window, let in some fresh air. It will pass within thirty minutes—your feelings, your energy is changing, they are resetting and this is just the adjustments working through your being.

## 11/

Get up and come straight to your notes. Write down all that you've seen and felt—this written download helps to avoid the mental analysis by your mind. The detail is in the messaging of your intuition and the strangest parts will prove themselves later down the line.

The colors of outfits, horses or the landscape will be key to what you need to do next, and of what your intuition requires of you as well as which crystal to carry to continue the filtering of your energy.

These are the meanings of the colors you intuitively flowed with:

**Blue/black:**
Relief and protection is here for you now—surrender to it.

**Red/orange:**
You are now held lovingly in your power. Release the memory of what was and accept what now comes to be.

**Purple:**
Time to be bold and brave. Spiritual awakening/recognition in the making.

**Green/brown:**
Tend to yourself through the heart you are growing—take time to ground and fully heal beyond the memory of what was. Focus on tending to your growth and planting seeds for the new, the next.

**Yellow/gold/white:**
Do not rush, take time to be still, listen to the silence beyond yourself.

**Pink/silver:**
Let it be—do not force, connect to what is, let go of how it should be and allow what can be.

**Rainbow of colors:**
You are endless, radiating possibility
—embrace it.

## THE REEL REVIEW

We often want to pick apart the messages from intuition, from the universe, and decipher them from the moment they've been given. But it is vital to use intuition's messages to untether from the pressure you put on your life and your future so that you can lean back into trusting that life and the universe holds you powerfully and lovingly here. Allow their meaning to take shape in their own time. The healing power of your intuition is to allow you to be able to view the hurt or the pain and to honor it. Not to relive it, but to shape it into something that is powerful to carry bravely, rather than sink under the weight of.

# For Finding
# Your Truth

W hat's your truth, like really? How do you know when you are lying or pretending to yourself? How do you recognize and make peace with those times when you went against your gut or intuition? How do you distinguish between your ego, which is so set on winning, or your intuitive tells, which are showing you how to move toward what's best for you? How often do we blame our intuition for getting it wrong when we just tried to lock it in the cupboard? Usually we do this because we think we are keeping ourselves safe, to avoid change and growth, or when we feel so desperate about getting what we want that we jump out of the intuitive frying pan (where we are cooking nicely) and into the fire of our ego.

# STORYTELLING

I have picked myself back up time and time again with this meditation that I like to call storytelling and I have strengthened my recognition of my intuitive "NO" versus my mind or ego's "NO" and my intuition's "YES" versus my ego's "YES." I use it still now when I am triggered—when someone mistakenly makes a move that sends me back into a fear of my past or when I feel frozen, unable to make a decision because I doubt or have lost fear in my truth. Then there is really only one thing for it . . . lying on the floor, kicking and screaming like a child!

1/

Come to your sacred space and let your body shake out as it needs to. Take to lying on the floor and have a tantrum like a spoiled child until you cry or laugh—either way you are breaking through. Then I verbalise the madness, screwing my face up tight and, as I exhale, I let all the tension go. Sometimes I sigh, sometimes I scream—whatever way you can surrender properly, completely, to the floor.

2/

Now it's time to soothe the hurt child with a guided intuitive healing story.

3/

Place your left hand on your inner compass, your solar plexus, right at the center of your belly and turn to lay on your right side on the floor (or the other way round, if that's right and comfortable for you. Lead by your dominant hand). You could even lie on your side under your duvet in bed with your hand on your belly, reading this like a meditative bedtime story that is guiding you home.

4/

Take the breath to your belly, fill it up huge like a bagpipe—in through the nose and exhale deeply from the belly out through your open mouth.

5/

With every breath, your mind will try to tighten. Let it—as with life, it tends to feel worse before it lifts to a shade of better. When it feels hard, mentally or emotionally, always move back to the breath as your anchor. Watch or feel your hand rising with that breath, coming back into that body beyond the wrongdoing or error and the anger dancing out and inside of you.

6/

Allow your eyes to move within, to the belly, into your depth, back to your power center and to where intuition fuels you. It'll perhaps feel dark, but with every breath you will start to feel the softening or a golden light dancing on your face. That's the energy of your intuition breaking through. Visualize, sense or feel green roots breaking through the darkness— with every inhalation, these roots are growing, filling you. With every exhalation, your attention moves as you visualize ash from a burned-out fire dancing in your belly—this is nothing more than the energetical remains of the dark, the anger moving out from the depths of you until the roots fill that space. Watch as these roots start to come to life. Then let them go, let them grow.

7/

With every breath, you are communicating to your intuition and the earth beneath you that holds you safe and steady that you trust these roots are affirming your place on this earth. That these roots are lovingly bringing life to where your intuition shows you the scar has been. These roots may wander in front of a memory of a pain or toward a time in which you had been happy in among the pain (remember intuition always seeks the good even in the hardest of situations). Take that feeling and allow it to grow with the intuitive roots to your mind's eye, to your place of ultimate creation and where you arrive in your mind's eye to a space where you can feel safe.

8/

This is a stage for you and your intuition to rehearse and to play out, but not yet act on your desires. Here you can see once more what feels right and grow the confidence once again to trust in it.

9/

Your mind will interject, terrified once again of making bad decisions, but focus on the roots and the life you give them with every breath as intuition fills you with the feeling of what is to come. In time, the person who embodied that feeling or bad decision will stand at the door of your place, between you and your light, casting shade. Give yourself permission to ask them to stand aside and to move them into that light— allow intuition to heal that place in your mind where they squatted.

10/

Before you now step into that light too, connect with your highest self. You read it, you say it, you accept it and it is done. You move into the light to bathe in it as you let your intuition take you to where you belong, whether you see it, sense it or know it. The light floods back in through the door into the entire body and your intuitive roots channel that light to every corner of your being of your body. Allow the electricity to fill you—in a moment you will close your eyes and when you do, you close that light in, allowing yourself to fly where your intuition needs and wants to take you—into your place of ultimate completion, showing you where you need to be and what your truth is now. Take a cleansing breath in through your nose, out through your mouth, close your eyes—now let your intuition allow your mind here to fly.

Don't set a time on this. Follow the story for the visualization for as long as your eyes stay open and beyond, when your eyes close. It will lead you to take your intuition by the hand once more and connect to it so you can conclude your story and see what you really want. When you are ready, allow your breath to bring awareness back into the body and the room. Have a glass of water then note what you saw and what you felt; what you were shown and how that felt for and to you—you bring it to life by speaking it.

5

•

# CARING FOR
# YOUR INTUITION

•

This chapter is for those times when you feel you can't, but your intuition knows you can. It's for when the fear sneaks up on you and you need to reset. In creating a healthy internal environment to heighten your connection, you will become more powerful and so will your intuition. It's also about the internal and external support that you can provide for your body and your intuition—to give your complete self a happy home to live within and for your mind, body and spirit to flourish.

As you now know, it's important to keep your energies clear and cleansed to ensure you get the greatest flow, but it's also important that we tend to the body in its entirety, not just to the parts of our body we are now using with our intuition as tells, because our body is the hero in all this working—the body is the flute that intuition uses to make its sweetest sound.

So how do we cleanse the flute—keep the instrument of self, happy and healthy? How do we allow ourselves to find its power on the grayest of days, when our happiness can seem far beyond our own control? Well we take a break . . . yup thats right . . . we bathe, we soak, we ground, we recharge, we affirm and then re-affirm. And we allow others to help support us and we take intuition by the hand and let it lead us to who, what and where those radiant beams are so that we can trust (perhaps trust *again*) heal more deeply and love full flow.

# For Recharging, Realigning, Reviving

Our body is the transmitter for our intuition and our intuition is only as good and as strong as the vehicle it resides in. When we calm the mind, the body can take a while to catch up and we may feel that it becomes harder to get back into our intuitive flow. I'm going to give you an intuitive break because you've been working harder than you realize and it's time to rest!

So, let us lighten the load by expanding on the mirror, mirror ritual from the previous chapter (see page 154) and applying it to the whole beautiful body, using the power of water to empower not only our mind, but our body.

●

# Your intuition is only as good and as strong as the vehicle it resides in.

●

## RESET WITH A GOOD SOAK

Water in itself is healing and soothing—remember our elemental power! So submerging under the water in the bath is one of my ultimate recommendations for anyone in the midst of a battle or in need of a little spiritual TLC. It's where I go when session work has been heavy and I feel a little out of myself, if I've encountered some drama or if someone else had thrust theirs upon me, or even when I have felt a strong reaction to the actions of another, or to celebrate myself when I have been working hard.

You may think that a bath is an obvious choice, but we are going to take the elemental power of water and mix in some more of Mother Nature's beauties to lighten and lift the load. It's time to add some energetical magic to your bath to calm both your body and mind, and heighten your intuition. Here is a magical mix of bath soaks that will sing to your mood—choose intuitively, based on where you are at rather than where you (or your ego) wants to be. If you are feeling angry, for example, use the "I speak" or "I love" soak coming up.

We will use nature's gifts in the form of salt and water. Salt is a purifier and can suck up worn or heavier energies, and we amplify this by mixing it with the soothing cleaning shifts made by water. We will use salt and water in all these mixes together with essential oils and crystals along with some magic words to bring your intuition back to prime position as the clearest voice in your internal house.

If you don't like getting in the bath or don't have one,

fret not—bathing your feet is just as powerful as bathing the whole body because the base of your feet is a map of the body's ecosystem and by releasing stress and tension there, you are tapping into an emotional, energetical detox for the entire body. We really are very magical!

Remember—these soaks are for taking a break. Aligning, calming and soothing your being, they should not feel like hard work but if you can't be bothered, then check back in with intuition and ask yourself why? Why can you not be giving of yourself right now? Let nature soak away the worries and align your being for you.

## SOAKS FOR EVERYDAY MOODS

### I AM

"I am" is the most powerful word combination in the history of all things, mainly because everything we create about ourselves begins with this: I am brave, I am brilliant, I am divine or, more commonly, I am sad, I am ugly, I am not who I want to be. We give them power by using them to define ourselves and this is then programmed into our psyche, ready for our ego to play out to us on repeat. Here is a mix to dissolve that programming, when this chatter has left you feeling on the edge, when survival mode is switched to red alert. Use this blend to return to yourself.

- Fill your bath with water set to a temperature most to your liking.
- Into the water, pour a cup of Himalayan or Epsom salts.
- **Add:** a mixture of 2 drops of each of these essential oils: geranium, rosemary, ylang ylang or sandalwood with 2 tablespoons of almond or argan oil as a base.
- **Place:** your crystals red jasper, ruby, garnet or bloodstone into your bath water or on the side of the bath (follow your intuition). If you only have one or two of these thats OK; use them—if you have them all—it will be a bonus, so please use where you can.
- Stir the water with your hand or arm and as you climb into the bath, unwind with your breath and affirm three times:
- **Affirmation:** "I am brilliance unwinding. I am kindness, love, the light of my own life."

## I FEEL

A bathing blend for when you're feeling like a puddle of water—stagnant and drained, with your energy evaporating under the heat of life. This is a soak for when you are low in self-respect or at either end of the emotional spectrum—underwhelmed or over-emotional. Use this mix to cleanse and soak away the negative feels and reconnect with your own sunshine.

- Run your bath to a temperature most to your liking.
- Into the water, pour a cup of Himalayan or Epsom salts.
- **Add:** 2 drops of each of these essential oils: neroli, rose, orange or sandalwood with 2 tablespoons of almond or argan oil as a base.

- **Place:** your crystals (two or all of the following): carnelian, calcite, citrine and topaz into your bath water or on the side of the bath (follow your intuition).
- As you climb into the bath, unwind with your breath and affirm three times:
- **Affirmation:** "I balance, I flow and I allow my emotions to intuitively guide me which way to go."

## I CAN

This is a real magic dip for when your worth feels as though it's been called into question or your mind is sinking into a guilt trip—get into this soak! Equally this is a mix for when you need to balance your intellect and clear your mind so you can tap into your intuition or to come down from a day of heightened stimulation (whether related to tech, an infant or the TV). It's also good when you need to reconnect with your self-confidence or reaffirm boundaries and build your self-esteem.

- Get your bath ready—fill it with water to a temperature most to your liking and into the running water, pour a cup of Himalayan or Epsom salts.
- **Add:** a mixture of 2 drops of each of the following essential oils: rosemary, peppermint, chamomile and marjoram, with 2 tablespoons of almond or argan oil as a base.
- **Place:** your crystals citrine, calcite, tiger's eye and amber into your bath water or on the side of the bath (follow your intuition).
- As you climb into the bath, unwind with your breath and affirm three times:
- **Affirmation:** "I can be all-powerful, all-balanced, all-intuitive me."

## I LOVE

Bathing in love allows us to bathe in forgiveness for ourselves and others, to promote compassion and to bring our self-control into balance. To bathe in this mix is to soothe in the acceptance of self or to warm your world when your nature has turned cold.

- Run your bath, pouring a cup of Himalayan or Epsom salts into the water as it fills.
- **Add:** a mixture of 2 drops of these essential oils: rose, rosewood, poppy, holly, jasmine and bergamot with 2 tablespoons of almond or argan oil as a base.
- **Place:** your crystals aventurine, rose quartz, jade, moss agate and pink tourmaline into your bath water or on the side of the bath (follow your intuition).
- As you climb into the bath, unwind with your breath and affirm three times:
- **Affirmation:** "In love I am, in love I understand—be it for me or all those who have love for me."

## I SPEAK

This is a mix for when you are seeking to tap into your patience to calm your human voice. It allows you to express yourself powerfully when you feel you are being suppressed, to hear yourself when others aren't listening. It's a soak for communication, expression, talking with your intuitive filter or for drawing you out of your snail's shell when you've been introverted and quiet for a little too long.

- Run your bath, mixing a cup of Himalayan or Epsom salts into the water as it fills.
- **Add:** a mixture of 2 drops of these essential oils: geranium, sage, lemongrass and juniper, with 2 tablespoons of almond or argan oil as a base.
- **Place:** your crystals lapis lazuli, topaz, blue lace agate and larimar into your bath water or on the side of the bath (follow your intuition).
- As you climb into the bath, unwind with your breath and affirm three times:
- **Affirmation:** "I patiently surrender to nurture my flow in order to allow my intuitive voice to stand tall and grow."

## I SEE

This is a mix for the sixth sense, to reveal your intuition by relieving hidden or repressed emotions, negative thoughts, overactive imagination or a lack of trust in yourself and the universe. In return it allows the energetical lens through which you look at yourself and life to clean up, showing yourself as you truly shine.

- Run your bath to a temperature of your liking, mixing a cup of Himalayan or Epsom salts into the water as it fills.
- **Add:** a mixture of 2 drops of these essential oils: peppermint, lavender and rosemary, with 2 tablespoons of almond or argan oil as a base.
- **Place:** your crystals amethyst, selenite (for the side of the bath only as it is water-soluble), sodalite and sapphire

into your bath water or on the side of the bath (follow your intuition).

- As you climb into the bath, unwind with your breath and affirm three times:
- **Affirmation:** "And now it's time for me to see, the greatest version of life for me."

## I KNOW

This is a blended bath mix to heighten connection when you're feeling a lack of it. When you are growing your relationship with intuition, you are empowering yourself and changing internal patterns of the mind as well as externally tweaking friendships and values if they no longer feel right—and that means you have to dissolve a lot of the old to embrace the new. Being fully in your intuitive flow means you can trust without fear. So this is a soak for when you over-analyze—and not in a good way—or when you feel spiritually deflated, tense and lacking in joy. It's also for when you are ready to lift your energies, your connection to the universe, to intuition and to yourself even higher, and bathe in your glory because you've worked your intuitive muscle hard.

- Run your bath to a temperature most comfortable to you, mixing a cup of Himalayan or Epsom salts into the water as it fills.
- **Add:** a mixture of 2 drops of these essential oils: sandalwood, neroli, lavender and rose with 2 tablespoons of cedarwood, almond or argan oil as a base.

- **Place:** your crystals clear quartz, selenite (by the side of bath rather than in the bath because it is water-soluble), howlite and Herkimer diamonds in your bath water.
- As you climb into the bath, unwind with your breath and affirm three times:
- **Affirmation:** "I know that life is unfolding and evolving all around me, and I trust in the connection and timing of my life as it does."

Remember these are soaks that move you into a more intuitive state of being, so it is more than likely that you will receive guidance or signs in the bath from intuition at this time—your mind's eye will open, your body will become more alert—listen in to intuition's voice as if playing music and tapping into its vibe and stream. If so, write them down once you are out of the bath and take time to sit with what you have sensed, seen or felt when you have time to take in your sacred space.

# For Releasing Fear and Doubt, and Managing the Mind

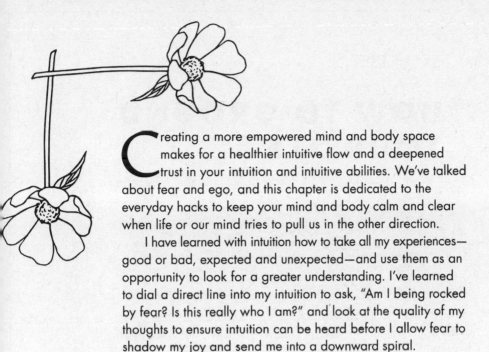

Creating a more empowered mind and body space makes for a healthier intuitive flow and a deepened trust in your intuition and intuitive abilities. We've talked about fear and ego, and this chapter is dedicated to the everyday hacks to keep your mind and body calm and clear when life or our mind tries to pull us in the other direction.

I have learned with intuition how to take all my experiences— good or bad, expected and unexpected—and use them as an opportunity to look for a greater understanding. I've learned to dial a direct line into my intuition to ask, "Am I being rocked by fear? Is this really who I am?" and look at the quality of my thoughts to ensure intuition can be heard before I allow fear to shadow my joy and send me into a downward spiral.

## GROUNDING

Intuition uses our body as its favorite tool, but so do anxiety, doubt and fear. Remember these are not parts of you that need fixing nor parts that we can remove as such, but we can learn to hear what fear sounds like in contrast to intuition and we can walk with fear rather than letting it drag us into hiding. We can learn to hand anxiety over to our intuition too, so that we can treat it with the love and the kindness it deserves.

Being grounded means to be present in real time and it's super-useful for when fear takes us down a wormhole of worry and self-doubt.

# HOW TO GROUND YOURSELF

It's important that we learn how to do this standing up so we can use it on the go, feeling the power of yourself and your body in life at that moment, but you can also do this exercise lying down—if I've had a hard day, I will ground my body as I lie in bed to calm my mind and prepare for as peaceful a sleep as is possible. If the day feels as though it is running away before me and I am trying to catch up with it, I ground myself, remembering that I run the day, I don't race it.

1/

Come to standing, with feet hip distance apart. Stamp your feet on the ground to feel the ground beneath you.

2/

Bending gently at your knees, roll gently forward down to the ground, so that your fingers reach down to your toes (or as far as they can). Run your fingertips from your toes, up the front and backs of your legs—let your fingers move across the front and back of the legs, all the way up your body, up the belly, up the back, (as best you can). Run your fingers up the chest, across the shoulders, up the neck, front and back, across the face, back of head, all the way to the top of your head till you come back to standing. Don't worry about being precise, it's more about creating a sensory awareness of the shape of your entire body.

3/

Roll your shoulders three times back then forth. Shake out your hands and fingertips before gently bringing your arms to stillness, slightly away from the sides of your body.

4/

Check in with your spine by taking a long inhalation in through the crown, the top of the head and, as you exhale out through mouth, move the breath and your awareness down along the spine, watching it elongate as you do so. Repeat three times.

5/

Looking ahead now, gently close your eyes (you can do this practice with eyes open and look ahead of you as you learn). Turn to your mind's eye or third eye and begin to visualize or sense roots or shoelaces (or whatever tie or binding material comes to you intuitively). Watch as these roots start to grow out from the base of your feet deep into the ground, right down, sinking deep into the warmth of the earth's core.

6/

Visualize a column of silver light or energy moving into your body through your crown. Use your breath to direct this energy down through your spine and connecting eventually with your choice of roots. Sense and feel as this light continually pours through you, running down through your roots into the ground, into the earth's core beneath you.

## 7/

Your body will start to sway as it grounds itself. Allow it—you will not fall. Allow your intuition and energy to fill your beautiful body and let intuition take the driving seat.

## 8/

If you are feeling anxious, doubtful or fearful, with each breath, allow that feeling to be drawn out of your body by the light, down toward the feet, to be neutralized by the earth. Allow yourself to be held by this invisible energetic force and the power of you and of your body. Allow any harsh language, cruel tones or mistruths to rise up for your acknowledgment only, and draw these fears, worries or criticisms down through your roots, down to the earth, where they are neutralized with no judgment or fear.

## 9/

At this moment, you just need to be at one with your intuition—take that time and you will feel safe, held and strong. Let that feeling grow out from you, creating a force field all around you.

## 10/

When you are ready, affirm in your heart and in your mind, that "I am totally safe, totally protected" before gently opening your eyes. Stretch out your body, take your arms over your head, perhaps you also come to the tips of your toes—feel what your body needs and explore it.

This feeling of safety is really good if you have been rocked by fear—it's like a strong, internal hug, but it's also an amazing place to come to when you are feeling calm and strong—you don't have to wait for ego to strike to reach out for this support!

You can also expand this grounding practice and pull in practices from this book—by perhaps using your intuitive tells from the first exercise (see page 45) and asking your intuition about what's led you here today, "How do I need to respond to my fear here in order to let it go?" or "Am I doing a good job?"

In order to dive deeper, simply repeat the exercise as above and as you come into step 10 and that point where there is nothing but you and intuition in the world in that moment, you can ask what is needed for you at this time and check in with your tells. Intuition will also flag other exercises in this book that you need to go back to in order to heal the situation, settle your energy or dive deeper into the answers to your questioning. For example, if you check in with your tells and ask, "Is this mine?" or "Is this someone else's?" when you are having a hard day and intuition tells you that it is another's energy that is causing you to feel out of sorts, dive back into the circle of light to look deeper and investigate why this has become the case. Or perhaps if you feel you have made a wrong decision you could ask of intuition how best to heal and move forward.

But if fear hits again and you are feeling vulnerable or shaken, that's more than OK; simply repeat the grounding exercise as often as you need throughout the day and wait to expand your intuition until you are back in your sacred space, after finding comfort perhaps in a bath soak (see page 200) or the chakra energy cleanse (see page 96).

This is such an important tool to carry when you are out and about, or even before bed. It won't give you instant answers or revelations because fear and anxiety can be complex and even debilitating, but grounding yourself in the everyday

can help us start to remember and feel our true sense of self and the power of that, in preparation for our intuition to heal us. With practice, you will be able to plug into that grounding feeling simply by stomping your feet with that intention, flowing with the breath and rooting in. I have done so in meetings and in interviews—I once had an experience on live television where the fear rushed toward me like a ghost in a haunted house saying "You are going to freeze" and "You're going to mess this up." Terror tried to shake through me, but I took charge. I felt for my feet, came to my breath and with intuition we moved the noise of my fear right back and allowed my intuition to fly forward—it was a really brilliant interview and I even managed to enjoy it!

## OTHER WAYS TO GROUND YOURSELF

My first recommendation is to get back in touch with the real world and by that I mean looking to nature rather than your phone. There is so much energy flowing through us and around us that we need a grounding wire to balance ourselves. We can do the previous grounding exercise barefoot on the grass or soil, or lean against or sit under a tree to feel nature's support and her magnetic field in our intuitive workings—the roots of the tree supporting our own roots to earth. As you do this, be mindful of the texture of the tree bark, the grass at your feet, the clarity of the fresh air in your lungs, the noise of the birds. Close your eyes.

I also use my breath and the scent of essential oils—use scents that uplift you or that you are drawn to intuitively. Raise your hands to your nose, take a deep inhalation in, breathe that scent in, lower your hands as you exhale and repeat three to five times.

I carry a menthol inhaler stick with me; when I start to feel short of breath or that my mind is racing, I use it to help me to come back to my body and take to the breath, breathing in for six and out for seven, affirming always in my mind with my intuition that "I am totally safe, I am totally protected."

## EDITING YOUR THOUGHTS

Our ego can throw some serious obstacles at us and our mind can loop our ego's voice over and over into our subconscious. However, our intuition can tell or alert us to when we are in such a loop and we can work with it to catch and then edit these thoughts. Meditation is an incredible tool for dialing inward and watching our mind's thoughts, clearing our mind to help power our intuition while reducing the noise of our ego—all of the practices or meditations in the book will help you to heal these patterns and habits over time, and we can also ask intuition to flag these loops daily, so that we can work with it to change the message for good.

By learning
to ground
ourselves we
can tune in to
intuition and
ask what's
happening.

# INTUITION FOR EDITING OUR EVERYDAY THOUGHTS

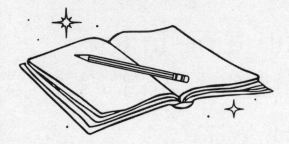

This is great for when you are on the go or even sitting in front of the TV. All you will need to do is dial in to your intuition as you would in your sacred space. For now, we will practice in our sacred and safe spot!

Sitting in your sacred space, once again come to a cleansing breath, inhaling for a count of seven and out for a count of six (both in and out through the nose). Repeat three times. Call forth your intuition through the circle or dial, or as you sense or feel it best. With intuition now holding your heart and hand, say to it "I ask and trust in you to give me a tell, to alert me to when my mind, my thoughts are treating me unfairly, are being unkind." Repeat three times and allow yourself to sense, feel and become aware of how intuition will signal this to you. Accept it.

When you are now in your everyday and you receive your tell or intuition leads you to notice the state of your thoughts, state out loud or in your mind "I catch that thought and I cancel it, I heal it" and, like a file on a computer, we can overwrite it by saying "and I replace it with . . ." (as an example, when I am critiquing how I look, I replace it with "Emma you are perfect and whole, you are exactly how you need to be."

This is a really important everyday ritual and over time you will come to accept that you deserve the loving thoughts in your mind and that it's OK to think kindly, positively and lovingly of yourself and even another.

## THE POWER SMILE

Sometimes we need the magic of the chemicals in our body. I know how much joy I get from laughing and I understand how the release of endorphins into the body, triggered by the muscles in your face, release these great chemicals to make us feel happy and to release stress. When I feel as if I have nothing to smile about and when even intuition can't move me, I remember the power of a smile to lift my mood—my power smile—even if I don't feel like laughing.

So why not add the words "power smile" as an intention card or as a reminder on your phone or calendar to help you to reduce the power of fear and of your ego, and to ease the flow of your intuition? And then you smile and you take it wide, as if it's stretching your mouth from ear to ear. It will feel a little forced, perhaps a little overstretched at first, but it will soften as you remind your face what it feels like to hold this here. You can hold it for thirty seconds or three minutes if you can, time isn't important—the action and the intention are. And for an extra sweet sleep take this smile with you as you close your eyes and lay in bed, headed into a slumber.

## GIVING THANKS AND COUNTING OUR BLESSINGS

Giving thanks and counting our blessings at the end of the day is super-important. Consider it another opportunity to sink into your intuition and raise your vibration to the universe.

Recite to your intuition, either in your mind or aloud, the top ten events of your day, good or bad. Give thanks for the positive ones—the blessings—and especially for the ones where you didn't respond quite how you might have wished. Say, for example, "I really lost my cool/

my ego got the better of me and if I could do it again, I would handle it better. I would take the space to cool down, walk away and listen to my intuition before responding." Let the conversation flow freely, let your words and your voice do the talking. Be thankful that intuition is there showing you where you can grow, rather than taking these thoughts to sleep with you. The brain is a powerful thing—it will register these last moments and save them into your internal hard drive, sinking them into your psyche. You own your mind, it doesn't own you, so take control of it before you go to bed each night.

You own your
mind, it does
not own you.

# For Health and
# a Happy Home

T he atmosphere around us is as important as the atmosphere within us for our intuitive care. Some energies are within our control, some are a little harder to manage.

Let's start with the most important—your home.

Your home is an extension of your self. Consider the rooms or spaces you favor and how you feel the warmth and love embody you as soon as you roam into these spaces. Intuition will always take you to these places to nurture you and to warm you. As with your sacred space, it thrives in them and it will lead you away from those spaces that can feel heavy or turn your mood gray when you step into them. That energy lingers in the atmosphere and it can have an effect that we can so easily confuse as our own. It's hugely important therefore to keep the energies in your home fresh and clean, so when tension appears, you need to cleanse the energy quickly as you would mop up a glass of spilled wine before its stain settles in.

As with cleansing your sacred space or yourself, use white sage or palo santo. Remember that sage is a little tougher— I find it good on the tough stuff and turn to palo santo for gentle or delicate work, but with maximum shine. Think of your energy like you do your washing—what temperature, what heat is needed for the quality of the wash, the delicacy, the color . . . your energy is no different.

Focus on the corners of the rooms because negative or

heavy energy tends to congregate there like dust balls—they gather, grow and have nowhere else to go! Take your smudge stick and lightly dust in the corners of the room from the floor up to the celling. With your intuition, set the intention, "I lift the energies that have become stuck and stagnant within my home and that hold me back from my maximum intuitive flow." Repeat three times.

I have a home studio for energy work and, once a month, I place a glass of water in each corner of the room for one week. This helps neutralize the wild emotions that I have worked from someone else, whose energetical echo has become caught in the walls.

Daily practices of lighting incense or candles will create satellite signals to the energy you have been nurturing within in your sacred spaces and you can send energy signals to the other rooms within your home—light a candle or incense stick in your sacred space and then light a candle or a incense stick in the rooms that require cleansing or an uplift—these will be your signal points for the energy to cleanse and flow. You can also go one step deeper—come back to your sacred space and move the room or office space through your mind's eye into the circle of light practice (see page 164) for intuitive healing, instead of seeing people moving into your light circle.

We can take it even further . . . yes we can! You can bring a talisman or symbol that represents your sacred space or the elemental energy to your place of work or into your car to transmit the energy even further. It will create that comforting and loving space for your intuition to amplify when you are away from your home—like a Wi-Fi extender!

Crystals are also brilliant for diffusing, filtering and cleansing energy naturally and will work on the energy in your home as well as from those people who enter your home. Here are a few crystal energy pairings that I recommend:

- Smoky quartz is what I call the hoover of negative energy and when paired with tourmaline, an energy-grounding stone, it will take the hoovered energy back into the earth for you.
- Just as you would have a doormat at your front door, place malachite at the entrance to your home alongside a piece of rose quartz to lovingly brush off any energy dirt from you or your guests as they pass the doorway. Malachite will powerfully scan and zap the bad energies on their way in and out of your house. Rose quartz is the queen of the heart and allows this cleansing to be done with love and for the highest good of all, welcoming and warming people as they come and go, and diffusing the malachite.
- Use your intuition to place other crystals around your home— you are a pro at this by now. Standing in a room, plant your feet on the floor so you ground yourself in the space. Open your heart to intuition and come to the breath. Ask of intuition, "What vibration would be best drawn into the room?" Your intuition will read the energy in the room and translate through a feeling delivered to your body. If love is required use rose quartz or another crystal that resonates with you as heart-centering—not sure which that is? Use your intuitive tells or cards. If clarity is needed, use clear quartz to boost the vibration to work toward clear conversations and intentions rather than quickly triggered arguments. Just like crystals, the vibe choices are endless.

- If you already have a crystal set that is currently on your bedside table, lay your crystals out before you in the room you are working on energetically. Use the energy center/chakra at the palm of your hand as you would your intention cards. Gently close your eyes and start to scan the crystals from left to right, back and forth, asking of your intuition and the crystals, "What do I want, what do I need?" Let the crystals communicate with your intuitive senses, feel for them as you do with your intention cards, allow for that pulse, that prickle or tell—let the crystals vibrate or pulse back to you. Once you have connected to the crystal, take it in your dominant hand, stand in the doorway of the room, ground your feet into the floor, let your arms gently hang by your sides and once again come to close your eyes. Place the forefinger of your free hand on your mind's eye or third eye and ask intuition to walk you around the room in your mind's eye, to show you where to place your crystal. If your mind gets distracted, come to the breath and repeat "I clear my mind, I see with intuitive ease." Sometimes it will come to you like lightening, sometimes it will take a little more time; take all the time that you need.

## OUT OF THE HOME—YOUR ENERGY SHIELD/BUBBLE

The energetic atmosphere beyond our home—in the supermarket, on the bus, on the pavement—can have such an impact on us too. Much as the environment around us can affect our skin and hair, it can also make an impact on our intuitive and energetical body. We've talked about energy from other people entering and perhaps throwing off the vibe in our home, so as you can imagine, spaces that are full of people will also be brimming with their energy.

You can join in that flow, adapting to the vibration of a rogue energy or fear, or you can bubble yourself in energetically to keep your energy fresh and be who you are, walking with peace and sunshine in the world.

- Before you leave the house (and this will become quicker the more you practice it), stand in your sacred space and visualize your energy roots once again growing out from your feet deep into the earth's core, as we do in the grounding exercise. Move your breath up and down your spine, feeling a connection of energy above you, moving through you and bringing life and power to your intuition at your core.
- Feel or visualize a yellow vortex of energy begin to spiral open at your gut. This is your intuition taking energetical form once more and with every breath this vortex of golden yellow light spins endlessly in front of you, creating a circular bubble, the shape of the sun. With your breath, blow into and expand that intuitive energy bubble—allow it to grow out from your core until it is bigger than your physical body.
- Your intuition is now embodied as light and is moving outward from you, but not leaving you, so take a physical step into the bubble, this shield.
- Feel the warmth of your intuition dance not only within yourself but also powerfully outside of yourself now. Feel the joy, the love and the peace stepping into that light and feel how it perfectly seals you in, but without any restriction.

- Use your intuition to connect with the universe and ask that this higher power now seals your intuitive bubble in with a blue or white light or what is shown or feels right to you.
- Affirm to and with intuition that: "I am totally safe, totally protected for the day before me and the road ahead of me." Repeat this three times and take a sealing breath in and out through the nose; with that you are ready to go.

It is better to practice these connections in your sacred space at first, but you will soon be able to "bubble in" anywhere by calling your intuition, just like when the rain falls and you have your umbrella at the ready. And when ego calls "I'm not getting this" or "It's not working" know that's the sweet spot, the tipping point where ego knows that you're just about to . . . move through it, with your breath, with your mantras, with your intuition and with your self!

Ask your intuition to set the signs that this is working for you in the day. Watch how people interact with you. Those filled with sunshine will glow or radiate to you and those who are vibrating at a lower level will move out of your way as if by magic. Notice how you can observe life more clearly and although you may still slip into funks, you have more space internally and externally to respond and work through. Most importantly, feel how strong the volume of your intention is and how clear it is as you stand in its light, and how its energy deflects any negative intent from others.

## TAKING DOWN YOUR SHIELD

When you return home, it's time to wash off the energy dirt or tensions of the day. The shower is the quickest way to do this, of course, though you can do it in your sacred space too.

- Allow the water to wash over your body and, as it hits the top of your head, feel the weight or worry, the energy dirt wash gently from your energy field and slide down into the plughole.
- As the water washes you clear, start to feel or sense as your intuitive light bubble begins to pulse at your lower back. This is the bubble starting to open from the base of your spine, reversing the process from the morning. It will open until it becomes a sun-shaped disc ahead of you and then spin and shrink back into your belly, your center.

If you don't have time to shower as you come in, head to your sacred space and follow the same simple steps, visualizing the water washing you from head to toe—intuition has you.

You can also smudge your body with sage or palo santo, or spritz an aura spray over you. You can ground the energy however you feel on the day—just lean into that because that is your intuition and you now have the tools!

# For Healing and Supporting your Mind, Body and Spirit

Intuition sings through our body, so it's crucial that we take the time to tap into our self-care and self-love—for the stronger our body, the stronger our intuitive receptors become and the quicker we take heed of the call of intuition. Maintenance is not just for when the going gets tough (and please don't leave your self-care until it reaches that point). For the best level of intuitive flow, intuition needs us to support our body.

Equally our intuitive self needs support as it grows within us. As we grow, we reshape and develop our needs, desires and values with our intuition, so we need to find balance from within but also support from without—our own human scaffolding, so to speak. It's not there to hold us up, but to hold us steady while we renovate or replace a brick of self or two. You could also see it as a gardener who is there to assist us in rooting up weeds from our spiritual garden. These are weeds that intuition has brought to light during these practices and that you are now ready to pull up but feel you need someone with a different skill or toolset to aid you.

Healing is not always easy, it can be light or heavy, it can take minutes or months. This chapter is dedicated to your external team-building and to the practices and treatments that I have experienced that have supported my intuitive journey. Use your own intuition to discern not only which treatment or practice works for you but also the practitioner, leaning into your intuition to help you choose. Always come back to your "what's my" tells to answer these questions.

## ACCUPUNCTURE/ACCUPRESSURE

Traditional Chinese medicine has been studied and practiced for thousands upon thousands of years—it's one of the oldest medicine systems and is as popular now as it ever was. The practice of acupuncture can really support you in releasing a number of physical, emotional and energetical aliments, allowing you to tap back into the flow of your body, to expand and empower your life force. The same techniques can be applied by pressure from the hands without the need for needles. For me—working with people so up close and personally—acupuncture is a game changer in supporting my bodily systems and functions.

## STRETCHING

There are so many powerful variations of yoga and stretch work, all with incredible benefits, so there will be one to fit your vibe! If a flow yoga with fast-paced movement doesn't work for you intuitively, try yin yoga. I practice this before I go to bed to move me into the right space (physically, emotionally) to connect with my intuition and spirit overnight and to release whatever I've been holding on to during the day. It allows you to improve your circulation and flexibility, reduces stress and restores balance in the mind, body and spirit, and it works the meridian lines used in traditional Chinese medicine and acupuncture.

Kundalini yoga is also a deep and thoroughly interesting practice, combining poses with mantras and some brilliant breathing exercises within the poses for one heavenly release.

## BREATH WORK AND MEDITATION

There are many breathing and meditation-based practices in this book to help you work with your intuition. These are two of my favorite tools and we can also work on their quality.

Breath work is powerful and there are many techniques and practices, all of which can influence your physical, emotional and mental states. I love the breath work practice I tap into when I'm singing and swimming—it allows me to expand and to fill up my system deep with fresh air, fresh energy. Also, by expanding the breath, we tap into the parasympathetic nervous system, calming our being as talked about earlier. We use the breath to massage our internal organs and soothe the body in order for us to reclaim our minds, so we can use it to connect with our intuition. You can practice breath work on your own but having someone lead these practices for you is a real bonus, so explore workshops and classes. Kirtan is a practice based on bringing in a greater sense of peace through chanting mantras and song—one to try for sure!

With meditation, remember it doesn't always have to be seated. Your meditative practices can take place running, in the gym, on a walk—it's all about what works for you. You could also seek out a weekly meditation group and work with someone you trust to guide you and heighten your intuitive senses while you continue to grow your own personal practice. Go discerningly, set the intention that the right group will work with your schedule and allow life and intuition to lead you there. If it doesn't, don't give up and remember this is an opportunity to understand what feels right or whose energy works for you, so come back to the intention to manifest the right place, space or group for you, online or out in the real world.

## ENERGY HEALING

There are so many forms and variations of energy healing to assist in the awakening, revitalization or removal of energy. These will assist you should you need to recover from depletion or should you wish to find a deeper sense of alignment, which can be great—or mildly overwhelming. Tune in to your intuition as you search for the one that suits you best.

Energy healing is so personal and loving. Sometimes the shifts can leave you feeling liberated but then throw you completely in the next session. Finding someone here that you feel you can trust and open up to (over time or immediately) is absolutely key.

I have experienced and can recommend intuitive healing, light healing, reiki, angelic and shamanic healing, crystal healing and theta healing, but look for other energy healings that your intuition may lead you to.

I like to write down as much as I can of what I saw or felt after these sessions and I encourage my clients to do the same. Intuitive insight may appear immediately or days or weeks later . . . let them come, let them flow.

## FACIALS, REFLEXOLOGY AND LED LIGHT THERAPY

I have put this trio together because I have had treatments that encompass all three and it's insane for all the right reasons!

Facials don't sound particularly spiritual, do they? You might be wondering if my ego led me to add them! But intuition reminds me that helpful practices don't have to be overtly or obviously "spiritual"—it's not about bracketing things into categories (that's ego) and intuition is unique to each of us. There are so many practices that can soothe and honor your mind, body and spirit, and heighten your intuition.

The human body is smart and our faces and our feet are like its maps. With the right technician working and massaging dedicated points on our body, we can alleviate tension, and move stagnation and blockages, allowing energy to flow freely once again and allow intuition back into control as we unwind the mind.

LED light treatment is something I stumbled on in a facial treatment. Initially for mood elevation, it's now something I lean to at the end of a cycle, whether physical or emotional.

## HYPNOTHERAPY

Sometimes I find meditation hard, especially during times where I need to be highly creative and I am putting too much pressure on my mind. I teach meditation too and I have a wardrobe of tools here to help, but even still, no matter how much I change the tool to distract the mind—be it candle light, breath work, sound bowls, yoga or running—I just can't find a way to let my mind off the leash and back into intuitive flow, or sometimes I'm just too tired and fancy a pampered support! At these times, I have found that hypnotherapy is my guardian angel. Talking with a hypnotherapist and working toward what is creating the stagnation at a mental level and then diving into a deep mental state (but where I am completely aware of what is happening) is liberating for me.

As always, I write it all down afterward for the intuitive guidance that is hidden at that point, but that shows itself in the following days and weeks.

## MASSAGE/BODY WORK

The body is an instrument and when it is squished up and held in one position for a prolonged time, you won't be able to make the noises or moves that you would like to make or perhaps as effortlessly as you know you can. That can make for too much tension and a lack of intuitive flow.

There are a lot of massages to choose from and I have

tried a lot. A couple of years ago, I decided to have a massage at least once a month because sometimes physical exercises made me a little hard emotionally and sometimes grumpy. Exercise is amazing for stress release and clearing my mind, but I learned that I needed to soften after the hard stuff—after punching a punch bag, lifting weights or exhausting the body—in order to find the balance.

Again, choose a massage (as well as a therapist) that sings to you. Some of us will thrive off the skills of a proper (and I mean proper) deep Thai massage, but it can be too intense for others.

Consider bringing in Mother Nature and her plant-based oils for an aromatherapy massage, using essential oils tailored to your mood or aches and pains.

I have an extra vertebra in my spine and suffer with scoliosis, which means I am more sensitive to massage and I can feel out of sync if I have the wrong type. Osteopathy is the dream but myofascial release massage (a fairly new find for me) is also one that should be looked at if you have a long-suffering injury or chronic pain, recurring injuries or tension building up from everyday life and modern-day technology (just check in to where your shoulders are now! Sitting up by your ears or nestled down away from them as they should be?). Fascia is a fascinating web-like structure that builds up and runs through our entire body, which can form and build up and then hold our body against its natural range. So it needs to be manipulated and "broken down" through massage to allow your body to tune back in to its greatest potential. It is also thought to hold old memory and emotion, so releasing here is super-liberating and can work toward lifting you to your greatest emotional potential too.

## SOUND HEALING

Sound healing, gong baths, crystal bowls and tuning forks— these are all music to your intuitive ears! Think about how noise affects you in the day—the tone of someone's voice, the vibration they bring to you (does it calm or irritate you?) or the power of a banging tune that brings good memories. All energy has a frequency and sound healing is no different. These practices are great for taking you to a safe place much deeper within, switching the mind off and allowing your mind's eye, your third eye, to really dance with your intuition.

As always, I suggest that you write down as much of what you saw or felt after these sessions—intuitive insight may be days or weeks ahead of where you are now.

## SPIRITUAL/PSYCHIC READINGS

Sometimes we can get stuck in a rut and the practices in this book or others feel difficult and frustrating, so we look externally for answers. This is fine, but always go in with intuition for guidance, affirmation or confirmation rather than allowing these practices complete control of the direction of the reading. Direction always comes from within and a great reader will journey with you. As with the work you do in these pages, be sure you are clear on what you want to ask and most importantly WHY you are asking, why do you want to know? To what end—ego's or intuition's? And if you don't like the sound of something in the reading, know that you have the choice to change or redirect the path so long as it's for your highest good.

PLEASE NOTE: Recommendations from friends and family (and me, see page 243) are valuable, but remember that what you are going through is always going to be different, so use intuition to connect with the practice you feel drawn to and to connect with your chosen practitioner—ask them questions and ask your intuition whether it feels right. Is this the person I should be working with? Too many people have tried a practice, only to reject it after one bad experience that may have been because of a mismatch with the practitioner not the practice, or because of ego trying to get you to run back into its grips.

# For When You Feel You are Getting It Wrong

This section is dedicated to reminding you of your brilliance and your power. Connecting with your intuition on some days feels like a marathon, on others an exhilarating sprint, but always remember it is not a race!

If you know that you have been or are putting off the exercises and the work, or if you are feeling like you can't be bothered, that is normally ego and fear and sometimes it can just be life. You can flow and push past it as best you can and intuition will meet you there. A little effort is better than none, though don't use that as another means of self-flagellation.

So, don't give up because you got it wrong or life feels hard or unfair (that's your ego sneaking in). This is the time when you should turn back in. Lots of people reach out to me when they feel life has fallen or is falling apart—and that's OK, don't get me wrong. I say to them, as I say to you now:

YOU HAVE GOT THIS.

You are smarter, stronger, braver than you know. You are learning, you are healing, you are undoing and coming back to the essence of who you really are, who you have always been—before you became what you were taught or allowed to be.

If you are angry, raging or sad and frustrated, take the time to tune in and ask intuition: why? Catch it before the fear catches you and it feels as if it's become impossible to rise up again. If the environment feels too loud to hear your intuition or your mind is too chatty, move! Move your body, use your breath to stimulate a change of states. I can often be found walking and asking out loud with my headphones on, pretending that I am on a call, when really I am connected in a very different fashion to my intuition and to the universe. Or I make a portable focus space wherever I am through talismans from my sacred space or a trusted crystal pal. The most important thing you can do is remember you are learning and within these pages there is enough stimulation for your intuition to help it to tend you with love.

Remember your toolkit—your intuitive GPS, your tells, your calls, your sacred space, your practices, your meditations. You have a vast set of skills now and, if it feels like hard work, know you are talking to ego.

Have FUN with your intuition. Don't try to complicate it, just get back into your flow. If you get angry at intuition, that's OK—it'll never leave you, so just sink into a healing bath or turn to an exercise in healing.

And on the days when you just don't feel like it, listen to that. That's intuition talking. It's very normal to move in deep and then away from our intuitive flow for, if we didn't know life without it, we wouldn't appreciate how special and magical life truly is with it.

●

# I unsubscribe right here and now from my own bullshit.

●

# CONCLUSION: BECOMING YOUR OWN GURU

In conclusion . . . well . . . the honest truth here is, there is no conclusion, for there is no end point. This is an intuition mission (a fun one) not a mind marathon and I believe that is a very good thing. We are ever-growing, ever-evolving, ever-blooming. Life is ever-constant and flowing and, like you, it's a life that should be explored in all its glory. You have leaned in and deep, even on your rainiest days and for that I thank you. You have listened, connected to your intuition and acted on it. You will at times lean away from it, but not against it, for intuition will never be your enemy—it's forever your loyal friend.

Always keep this close to heart—you have come to see that even on the toughest days, in those darkest moments, your intuition can be the light that guides you through that darkness. I know that it wasn't easy to get there, but you did and you will again, time and time again. When the light shines, dance in it and shine in it brighter—you know now you deserve it.

If you have been waiting for a final huge "ta-da" moment, know that there isn't one (that's ego's dream). Instead of one win, there is a series of wins, of moments, of cheers from your human, universal and intuitive supporters, so keep your ears, heart and eyes open for them and don't miss the sweet spots by fixating on one moment your mind has created in time. Instead spend some time in your sacred space, sitting with intuition and acknowledging your wins. Celebrate from the inside out—and watch how life claps back. Know that these successes come to you not always in gold and sparkle or medals and certificates; they come as you have healed, revealed and bloomed.

How you feel, how you let go and how you now stand in your highest power, as you honored that force and saw it in that wonderful life and world before you—they are the true wins in life and YOU with intuition have brought it all together. YOU! Let's just celebrate that for a moment right now, shall we?!

In all that you have learned about intuition, I hope you take this away as the sweetest point—that working with your intuition is not about being perfect or about perfection in yourself or in all other living beings. It is all about being good to ourselves and to others, to live a high-vibe, high-energy, intuitive life as an example, not an enforcer for others' change.

So, go well, use this book however you need and have fun with your intuition. It's time to fly higher than ever before, knowing that you know more than you think you know—you always did.

# RESOURCES AND FURTHER READING

For more information on me, to find me, to book
a session or just to ask a question—please visit me
at www.emmalucyknowles.com

Find me on social media @your_emmalucy

For further reading and resources, I have included
a list of some of my most trusted practitioners,
stockists, spiritual reads and tools on my website
at www.emmalucyknowles.com/resources

Please play with your intuition here, tune in and trust
your gut—it's a great place to play with your "what's
my yes" and "what's my no," to sense what or who feels
like they are resonating with you. Remember: what is
right for you will never pass you by.

# THANK YOU

I cannot quite believe I am writing my thank yous for my third book . . . mad, brilliant, amazing but more than anything the biggest sign that following your intuition and working with it really does create blessings and miracles in human form; for this book could not have happened without any of you reading this or those of you who I have had the pleasure to work with in all capacities. For your faith and belief, I thank you all!

To my mummy & daddy, thank you for all the sacrifices you made for me (especially the extraordinarily painful ones) even before I was born. I could never thank you enough, so I will show it every day as best I can. To Becky, super star sister and communication extraordinaire— you are the best. I hope one day you will believe in yourself as much as I do you. And also to Dolly: all you Knowlesters are pure legends!

To the almighty book squad: THANK YOU x1000! I was blessed to have not one but two birthing partners on this book, both brilliant in their own right. So to Celia, the sweetest of souls, thank you for your kind brilliance—I could not have done this without you, thank you for letting me be and for encouraging me beautifully all the way. And to Elen (EJ), you are a star—thank you for bringing me the opportunity to write the book of my dreams. To the design guru that is Lucy and to Liz, thank you for bringing intuition to life with your magic. To Laura as ever, you rock, thank you for starting this journey off all those years ago.

To all my loving and loyal friends, I love you and I THANK YOU. You know

THANK YOU

who you are: close your eyes and
feel it!

    To Chris, Tom, Lady P, T&M, Eric, Lily
and all those who have flown that I have
the extreme honor of connecting with,
thank you for your trust, your love, your
guidance and for never giving up on me
even when I had given up on myself.

# INDEX

Exercises are in *italics*

## A

abundance and gratitude
    31–32
acupuncture/acupressure 230
air 59, 62–64, 105
amazonite 147, 159
amethyst 120, 159, 183, 205
ametrine 120
anger, detoxing from 159
anxiety 123, 168, 209–14
auras 94
aventurine 159, 160, 183, 204

## B

bathing 105, 200–207
blessings, counting 31–32, 218
the body 43. *See also* self-care
body indicators. *See* "tells"
breath work 59, 60, 105
    *Feeling the tells* 79
    *Finding your tells* 46–53
    and grounding 214
    and meditation 231

## C

candles 41, 60, 64, 222
cards. *See* intention cards
careers: decision making
    134–39
celestite 147–50

chakras 93–95
    *The chakra cleanse and connection meditation*
    96–102
    *Cleansing your energy* 106–8
Chinese medicine 230
citrine 160, 183, 203
cleansing 88, 105
    *The chakra cleanse and connection meditation*
    96–102
    *Cleansing your energy* 106–8
    energy shields 227
    your home 221–24
clear quartz 120, 160, 176, 223
comfort zone 23–24, 69
communication: bathing soaks for
    204–5
connecting to your intuition 42–53
    *The chakra cleanse and connection meditation*
    96–102
connectivity, cycle of 63
crises and intuition 5
crystals 41, 120, 159–60. *See also* bathing
    and chakras 102
    *The circle of light* 165
    cleansing with 223–24
    *Correcting the memory film* 182–87
    inner child work 146–50
    *A letter on love from your heart* 175–78
    *Mirror, mirror ritual* 154–57
    *Reconnecting with your inner child*
    146–50
    *Taking it to the next level* 158–60

## INDEX

**D**

dalmatian stone 165
decisions 134–35
  Pulling your intention cards 136–39
decisiveness 117
doubt 209, 212
drains. See energy drains
dreams 115

**E**

earth 60, 62–64
ego 11, 14, 23–28
  interference from 57, 117, 214
  and procrastination 37, 113
  vs intuition 26, 27, 57, 71
Einaudi, Ludovico Islands 79
elemental power 58–60
  Finding your elemental symbols 62–65
emotions 94
  bathing soaks for 201–4
  someone else's 75, 82
  your own 74, 81–82
empowerment 199, 206, 209
endorphins 217
energy 85
  Cleansing your energy 106–8
  negative 105, 221–24
  universal. See universal energy
energy centers. See chakras
energy circles 64–65
energy drains 73, 76
  Feeling the tells 81
  workplace 87–88
energy fields 100
energy healing 232–33
energy network 93–95
energy radiators 72, 76
  Feeling the tells 80
  workplace 87
energy shields 224–27
environmental impact 224–25
essential oils 214. See also bathing and
    grounding
  massage 235
exercises
  Asking your intuition 56–57
  The chakra cleanse and connection meditation
    96–102
  The circle of light 164–70
  Cleansing your energy 106–8

Feeling the tells 78–83
Finding your elemental symbols 62–65
Finding your tells 45–53
How to ground yourself 210–14
Intention-setting ritual 120–24
Intuition for editing our everyday thoughts
    216–18
Intuitive viewing 140–41
A letter on love from your heart 175–78
Mirror, mirror ritual 154–57
Pulling your intention cards 136–38
Reconnecting with your inner child
    146–50
Storytelling 190–93
Taking it to the next level 158–60
Using your tells and taking them out in the open
    86–90
Visualization 114–17
What is my sign? 126–27

**F**

facials 233
fear 23–24, 26, 71, 154
  and grounding 209–13
  Mirror, mirror ritual 154–57
  Taking it to the next level 158–60
feet 78, 79, 201
fire 63, 64, 105
friendships. See relationships

**G**

good & evil: The story of two wolves 6
gratitude 31–32, 218
greatest self 11, 19
grounding 209–14
  Finding your tells 47, 49

**H**

healing 181
  Correcting the memory film 182–87
  energy healing 232–33
  Mirror, mirror ritual 154–57
  sound healing 236
  Storytelling 190–93
  Taking it to the next level 158–60
the "highest good" 7, 10, 19
highest self 11, 19
home 220–27
honesty 27, 28
hypnotherapy 234

I

incense 64, 222
inner child 63, 153
    *Reconnecting with your inner child* 146–50
inner voice 26, 28
    *Intuition for editing our everyday thoughts*
        216–18
intention boards 112–13, 116–17
intention cards 122–23, 129
    creating 47, 49, 120–24, 127
    *Pulling your intention cards* 136–38
intentions 119
    *Intention-setting ritual* 120–24
    *What is my sign?* 126–27
the internet 89–90
intuition 1, 2. *See also* inner voice
    asking questions 56–57
    benefits of 8–11
    communication with others 94
    connecting to 42–44
    in crises 5
    and decision making 134–35
    definition of 4–6, 19–20
    everyday intuition 70–83
    inner voice 26, 28
    and truth/honesty 27, 28
    universal energy 6–7
    vs ego 26, 27, 57, 71
    when things go wrong 5, 238–40
    and wishes 112–13
intuitive tells. *See* "tells"

J

joy: *Taking it to the next level* 158–60

L

labradorite 120, 183
learning spaces 39–41
LED light therapy 233
list making 113, 116
love 173–74
    bathing soaks for 204
    as a guide 23
    *A letter on love from your heart* 175–78
    *Taking it to the next level* 158–60
    tokens of 41

M

malachite 223
manifestation boards 112–13, 116–17

massage 234–36
meditation 214, 231–32
memories: *Correcting the memory film* 182–87
the mind and ego 24
mind's eye. *See* third eye
mirrors 154–57
moods: bathing soaks for 201–4
multisensory network 19
music 79

N

needs vs wants 10
negative emotions
    bathing soaks for 201–4
    *Feeling the tells* 78–83
negative energy 105, 221–24
negative thoughts 214
    *Intuition for editing our everyday thoughts*
        216–18
"No:" intuitive no 48–50

O

online forums 89–90

P

palo santo 105, 155, 221
    *Cleansing your energy* 106–8
parasympathetic nervous system 59, 231
past hurts, healing 181
    *Correcting the memory film* 182–87
peace, tokens of 40–41
Pearson, Joel 20
photos 41
pictures 41, 117
preparation 37
procrastination 37, 114

Q

questions, asking 56–57

R

radiators. *See* energy radiators
reflexology 233
relationships 7, 10, 27, 76, 163. *See also* social
        situations
    *The circle of light* 164–70
    *A letter on love from your heart* 175–78
    romance and love. *See* love
    and vibrations 94
    with yourself 145–50

# INDEX

romance. *See* love; relationships
rose oil 155
rose quartz 147, 155, 160, 165, 176, 223

## S
sacred spaces 38–41, 58–60
salt 200–206
science and intuition 20
selenite 183
self-care 88, 197, 229–37
    bathing 105, 200–207
    *Mirror, mirror ritual* 154–57
    *Taking it to the next level* 158–60
self confidence: bathing soaks for 203
self esteem: bathing soaks for 203
self respect: bathing soaks for 202–3
shields 224–27
showering 105
shungite 46
signs: *What is my sign?* 126–27
sixth sense 19
    bathing soaks for 205–6
smiling 217–18
smoky quartz 223
smudging 107, 222, 227
smugness 27
social media 89–90
social situations 85
    and negative energy 74–76
    *Using your tells* 86–90
sound healing 236
spirit element 63–64
spiritual/psychic readings 236–37
*Storytelling* 190–93
stretching 230–31
success 242

## T
talismans 41, 63–65, 222
technological interference 46
"tells" 43
    energy drains 73, 76
    energy radiators 72, 76
    everyday intuition 70–83
    *Feeling the tells* 78–83

    *Finding your tells* 45–53
    *Using your tells* 86–90
third eye 28, 48, 50, 97, 99, 100, 108, 111
    *Intuitive viewing* 140–41
    *Taking it to the next level* 158–60
thoughts 214
    *Intuition for editing our everyday thoughts* 216–18
tiger's eye 147
tokens 41
totems 40
trust 2, 8, 24
truth 28, 189
    *Storytelling* 190–93

## U
universal energy 6–7, 93–95
    connecting to 60, 93–95, 111
universal life force. *See* universal energy
the universe: spirit element 63–64

## V
vibes 94
visualizing
    *Feeling the tells* 80–83
    *Finding your tells* 47
    *Visualization* 114–17
voice within. *See* inner voice

## W
wants 11, 23–24
water 62–63, 105
    bathing in 105, 200–207
white sage 105, 221
    *Cleansing your energy* 106–8
wishes 112–13
wolves: *The story of two wolves* 6
workplace 87–88, 222
worry: *Taking it to the next level* 158–60
writing 116, 150
    *A letter on love from your heart* 175–78

## Y
"Yes:" intuitive yes 46–48, 50–53
yoga 230–31